The Universal Developer's Guide

Leveraging Python and C# for Cross-Platform Coding, Agile Development, and Cloud Integration

THOMPSON CARTER

Table of Content

TABLE OF CONTENTS

Introduction

In today's rapidly evolving digital landscape, the demand for applications that seamlessly function across multiple platforms has never been greater. With users accessing software on a variety of devices—smartphones, tablets, desktops, and more—it is crucial for developers to create applications that work smoothly and efficiently across these diverse environments. Cross-platform development is the answer, enabling developers to write code once and deploy it across a range of operating systems, including Windows, macOS, Linux, Android, and iOS. However, while cross-platform development offers significant benefits, it also comes with unique challenges, from managing platform-specific issues to ensuring consistent performance across devices.

This book, *The Universal Developer's Guide: Leveraging Python and C# for Cross-Platform Coding, Agile Development, and Cloud Integration*, is a comprehensive exploration of how to master cross-platform development using two powerful and widely-used languages—Python and C#. Through this guide, we aim to equip developers with the tools, knowledge, and best practices necessary to create scalable, efficient, and maintainable cross-platform applications. Whether you are building mobile apps, desktop software, or web-based solutions, this book provides valuable insights into how Python and C# can work together to address the complexities of modern software development.

Why Python and C#?

Python and C# are two of the most popular programming languages in the world today. Python is known for its simplicity, versatility, and vast ecosystem of libraries, making it an excellent choice for tasks ranging from data science and machine learning to web development and automation. C#, on the other hand, is a powerful language that excels in enterprise-level applications, offering robust performance, rich libraries, and integration with the Microsoft ecosystem, particularly through the .NET framework.

When combined, Python and C# provide a complementary set of tools that empower developers to build dynamic and high-performing cross-platform applications. Python can handle backend logic, data processing, and integrations with ease, while C# shines in building user interfaces and cross-platform applications through frameworks like Xamarin,

.NET Core, and MAUI (Multi-platform App UI). By leveraging the strengths of both languages, developers can create truly universal applications that run across mobile, desktop, and cloud environments.

A Modern Approach to Cross-Platform Development

Throughout this book, we will focus on best practices and strategies that facilitate efficient cross-platform development, with a strong emphasis on **Agile development** and **cloud integration**. Agile methodologies have revolutionized the way software is developed, promoting iterative development, continuous feedback, and adaptive planning. Agile practices ensure that developers can quickly deliver value to users, respond to changing requirements, and iterate on their products based on real-time feedback. These principles will be incorporated throughout the book, ensuring that you not only learn how to build cross-platform applications but also how to do so in a flexible, responsive, and efficient manner.

As cloud computing continues to play an integral role in application development, understanding how to leverage cloud services for scalability, reliability, and performance is essential. In the chapters ahead, you will discover how to integrate cloud services, use **microservices** architecture, and ensure that your applications can scale as needed. The cloud offers unparalleled flexibility in managing resources, handling traffic spikes, and improving app performance—all crucial factors when building cross-platform solutions.

What This Book Will Cover

This book is structured to guide you through every stage of the cross-platform development process, from the initial planning and setup to deployment and maintenance. Here's a brief overview of what you can expect:

1. **Foundations of Cross-Platform Development**: We'll start by laying the groundwork for cross-platform development, introducing the basic concepts, tools, and frameworks that make it possible to target multiple platforms from a single codebase.

2. **Python and C# in Cross-Platform Development**: You'll learn how Python and C# work together to form a powerful, complementary toolkit. This section covers how to use each language for backend and frontend development, as well as how to create APIs, manage databases, and integrate external services.

3. **Agile Development and Cloud Integration**: Discover how to implement Agile practices to manage your projects effectively and build cloud-integrated applications that scale effortlessly. We'll cover continuous integration and deployment (CI/CD), automated testing, and version control with Git.

4. **UI and UX Design for Cross-Platform Apps**: Designing user-friendly, responsive interfaces is one of the biggest challenges in cross-platform development. This chapter will help you tackle platform-specific UI issues, implement responsive designs, and use native device features across different platforms.

5. **Debugging, Troubleshooting, and Performance Optimization**: Learn how to identify, debug, and fix common issues that arise in cross-platform development, such as UI inconsistencies, platform-specific bugs, and performance bottlenecks.

6. **Deploying and Scaling Applications**: Understand how to package your applications for different platforms (Windows, macOS, Linux, Android, iOS) and deploy them to the cloud or on-premises. We'll explore deployment strategies, scaling solutions, and

how to ensure your application runs efficiently in production.

7. **Future Trends**: In the final chapters, we'll look ahead to the future of cross-platform development. We'll explore emerging trends like AI and machine learning, and how they are being integrated into cross-platform applications to create smarter, more responsive software.

Who This Book is For

This book is designed for developers of all levels who are looking to enhance their skills in cross-platform development. Whether you're a beginner who wants to learn the basics or an experienced developer seeking to expand your knowledge of cross-platform tools and methodologies, you will find practical advice, real-world examples, and detailed explanations throughout.

If you are already familiar with Python or C#, this book will deepen your understanding of how to leverage these languages to build cross-platform solutions. If you are new to these languages, the concepts introduced will provide a solid foundation upon which you can build more advanced knowledge.

What You Will Gain

By the end of this book, you will:

- Master the tools, frameworks, and best practices for building cross-platform applications.
- Be proficient in combining Python and C# to create scalable, efficient, and feature-rich applications.
- Understand how to implement Agile methodologies and integrate cloud services to ensure your applications are scalable and maintainable.
- Gain hands-on experience with debugging, troubleshooting, and optimizing cross-platform applications.
- Learn how to deploy applications to multiple environments and platforms, ensuring a seamless user experience across devices.
- Be ready to incorporate emerging technologies like AI and machine learning into your cross-platform apps.

In the ever-evolving world of software development, this book provides you with the knowledge and skills to build modern, scalable, and efficient cross-platform applications that will serve the needs of users across a wide range of platforms and devices. Let's dive in and explore the future of cross-platform development, powered by Python and C#!

CHAPTER 1

INTRODUCTION TO CROSS-PLATFORM DEVELOPMENT

Overview of Cross-Platform Development and Its Significance in Modern Software

Cross-platform development refers to the practice of creating software applications that can run on multiple operating systems and devices without requiring separate codebases for each platform. In today's fast-paced tech world, it's crucial for developers to build applications that work seamlessly across a variety of platforms, including Windows, macOS, Linux, Android, and iOS. This approach helps to save time, reduce costs, and improve the consistency of the user experience across different devices.

Cross-platform development is particularly important because users expect to have a consistent experience, whether they're accessing an app on their phone, tablet, or computer. Additionally, the explosion of different devices and operating systems in the market means that businesses and developers need to consider various platforms if they want their applications to reach the largest audience possible.

Importance of Using Python and C# for Cross-Platform Solutions

Both **Python** and **C#** are versatile languages that are widely used for building cross-platform applications. Each offers its own set of strengths, making them ideal candidates for cross-platform development:

- **Python** is renowned for its simplicity, ease of use, and a broad range of libraries and frameworks that enable developers to build applications quickly. It is often used for backend development, data analysis, and automation, but with frameworks like Kivy, PyQt, and BeeWare, Python can also be used to create graphical user interface (GUI) applications that work on multiple platforms.

- **C#**, on the other hand, is traditionally associated with Windows development but has evolved with the advent of **.NET Core** and **Xamarin**. These frameworks enable C# developers to create applications that run not only on Windows but also on macOS, Linux, iOS, and Android. C# is a robust language used for building everything from desktop software to web applications, and its cross-platform capabilities make it a powerful choice for developers looking to reach a wide audience.

Together, Python and C# offer a dynamic combination for developing both lightweight and enterprise-level cross-platform applications.

Brief on Agile Development Methodology and Cloud Integration

- **Agile Development Methodology**: Agile is a software development approach that emphasizes flexibility, collaboration, and iterative progress. With Agile, development is broken down into smaller cycles or sprints, where developers can deliver parts of the application and receive feedback quickly. This allows teams to adapt to changes more easily and ensures that the application evolves based on real-world usage and feedback. Agile is particularly beneficial for cross-platform development because it promotes frequent testing and adjustments, which is essential when working across diverse platforms.

- **Cloud Integration**: Cloud computing allows applications to leverage the power of remote servers for data storage, processing, and other backend services. Cloud integration makes it easier for developers to build scalable applications that can handle high volumes of users and data. It also ensures that data is accessible across different devices, providing a consistent experience for users no matter where they are or what device they're using. Cloud services, such as AWS, Microsoft Azure, and Google Cloud, offer extensive tools for developers to integrate cloud functionalities into their cross-platform apps, such as cloud storage, databases, and authentication.

Real-World Example: Cross-Platform Mobile Apps

A common real-world example of cross-platform development is the creation of **mobile applications**. For instance, consider a mobile app designed to help users track their fitness goals. By using a cross-platform framework like **Xamarin** for C# or **Kivy** for Python, developers can write a single codebase that runs smoothly on both **iOS** and **Android** devices.

This is beneficial because maintaining two separate codebases for iOS (using Swift or Objective-C) and Android (using Kotlin or Java) can be time-consuming and costly. With cross-platform development, the same functionality and UI can be shared across platforms, while still being customized for each device's specific requirements.

For example, a fitness tracking app built with **Xamarin** could be deployed to both the App Store (for iOS) and Google Play (for Android), with features such as syncing workout data to the cloud, push notifications, and integrating with third-party APIs like health and fitness devices. By using cloud services, users could have their progress saved and accessed across multiple devices (phone, tablet, or desktop).

This is just one of the many examples where cross-platform development, coupled with Agile methodologies and cloud integration, enables developers to build efficient, scalable, and high-performing applications that meet the demands of modern users.

CHAPTER 2

UNDERSTANDING PYTHON: THE VERSATILE LANGUAGE FOR DEVELOPERS

Python's Core Features, Strengths, and Ecosystem

Python is one of the most popular and versatile programming languages today, known for its simplicity, readability, and broad range of applications. Below are some of its core features and strengths:

- **Easy to Learn and Read**: Python's syntax is designed to be intuitive and closely mirrors human language, making it one of the best languages for beginners. Unlike some languages with complex syntax, Python is designed to be straightforward, reducing the barrier for new developers.

- **Dynamically Typed**: Python doesn't require you to declare the type of variable beforehand. The interpreter automatically handles the types based on the value assigned to a variable, which simplifies the development process.

- **High-Level Language**: Python abstracts away many of the low-level programming complexities such as memory management, making it easier to focus on solving the problem at hand rather than dealing with the intricacies of system-level coding.

- **Extensive Libraries and Frameworks**: Python has an incredibly rich ecosystem of libraries and frameworks. Libraries like **NumPy**, **Pandas**, and **Matplotlib** make Python a favorite for data science, while **Flask** and **Django** are highly popular for web development. Python's ecosystem allows developers to quickly integrate solutions without reinventing the wheel.

- **Versatile and General-Purpose**: Python can be used in almost any domain—web development, machine learning, automation, data analysis, scripting, and more. Its versatility is one of the key reasons Python is commonly used for cross-platform development.

- **Open-Source**: Python is open-source, meaning it's free to use and has a large, active community. The availability of open-source tools and libraries makes it easier to find support, share knowledge, and contribute to the language's growth.

20

Python's Role in Cross-Platform Development

Python plays an important role in cross-platform development due to its flexibility and vast selection of cross-platform tools and libraries. Some reasons Python is ideal for cross-platform development include:

- **Cross-Platform Libraries and Frameworks**: Python has frameworks like **Kivy**, **BeeWare**, and **PyQt** that allow developers to write code that can be deployed across different platforms without modification. These frameworks provide tools to build desktop and mobile apps with a single codebase that runs on Windows, macOS, Linux, iOS, and Android.

- **Portability**: Python itself is available for all major operating systems, and Python code can often run without modification on any supported platform. As long as the necessary dependencies are available, Python code can be executed on virtually any system.

- **Cross-Platform GUIs**: Python's support for cross-platform GUIs through frameworks like **Tkinter** (for desktop apps) and **Kivy** (for mobile apps) allows developers to create user interfaces that work across different platforms. This is particularly useful for

21

developers looking to create apps that are accessible to a wide range of users without needing separate code for each platform.

- **Platform-Specific Libraries**: For more advanced use cases, Python provides access to platform-specific libraries and system calls through **PyObjC** (for macOS) or **PyWin32** (for Windows). This makes it possible to leverage platform-specific features when needed, while still maintaining a cross-platform codebase.

Setting Up the Development Environment for Python

To begin using Python for cross-platform development, you'll need to set up a suitable development environment. Here's how to get started:

1. **Install Python**:
    - Download the latest version of Python from the official website: python.org.
    - Ensure that the Python installation adds Python to the system's PATH so you can run Python from the command line or terminal.
2. **Install a Code Editor**:
    - Popular Python editors include **VS Code**, **PyCharm**, or **Sublime Text**. These editors

provide features like syntax highlighting, debugging, and extensions for Python development.

3. **Set Up Virtual Environments**:
   - Virtual environments allow you to isolate dependencies for different projects, avoiding conflicts between packages. You can create a virtual environment by running:

```nginx
python -m venv myenv
```

   - Activate the virtual environment:
     - **Windows**:
       ```
       myenv\Scripts\activate
       ```
     - **macOS/Linux**: `source myenv/bin/activate`
   - Once activated, you can install necessary packages for your project using `pip`.

4. **Install Cross-Platform Frameworks**:
   - Depending on your project, you may want to install a cross-platform framework like **Kivy** (for GUI apps) or **Flask** (for web apps):

```nginx
pip install kivy
```

```
pip install flask
```

- o These frameworks will enable you to build applications that can run across multiple platforms with minimal modifications.

5. **Testing Across Platforms**:
   - o If you're developing for mobile or other platforms, set up emulators or physical devices to test your code. For instance, you can use **Xcode**'s simulator for iOS development or **Android Studio** for Android apps.

Real-World Example: Building a Simple Python App for Different Platforms

Let's take a look at building a simple cross-platform app with **Kivy**, a popular Python framework for creating multi-touch applications, including mobile and desktop apps.

Step 1: Install Kivy

First, install Kivy using pip:

```
nginx
```

```
pip install kivy
```

Step 2: Write the Code

Create a simple application that displays a button and prints a message when clicked.

python

```
from kivy.app import App
from kivy.uix.button import Button

class MyApp(App):
    def build(self):
        return Button(text="Click Me!")

if __name__ == '__main__':
    MyApp().run()
```

Step 3: Run the App

Run the app on your local machine by executing the Python file:

nginx

```
python myapp.py
```

This will open a window with a button labeled "Click Me!". When clicked, it will print a message to the console.

Step 4: Testing and Deployment

- To deploy the app to different platforms (e.g., Windows, macOS, Android), you can package it using **Kivy's build tools** or tools like **PyInstaller** for creating standalone executables. For mobile apps, you can use **Buildozer** to package and deploy the app to Android or iOS.

For Android:

- Install Buildozer:

```nginx
pip install buildozer
```

- Build the app for Android:

```nginx
buildozer -v android debug
```

This simple example demonstrates how Python can be used to build a cross-platform application that works on both desktop and mobile. By leveraging frameworks like Kivy, Python enables you to write once and deploy across multiple platforms, saving time and reducing complexity.

CHAPTER 3

MASTERING C#: A POWERFUL TOOL FOR CROSS-PLATFORM SOLUTIONS

Key Features of C# and Its Role in Cross-Platform Development

C# is a modern, object-oriented programming language developed by Microsoft, primarily known for its association with Windows applications. However, with the advent of **.NET Core** and **Xamarin**, C# has become a powerful language for cross-platform development. Here are some key features of C#:

- **Object-Oriented**: C# is inherently object-oriented, meaning it focuses on the concept of objects and classes. This makes it easy to model real-world entities in your code, allowing for clean and maintainable software development.

- **Rich Library Support**: C# comes with a vast standard library, offering everything from data structures to file handling, networking, and more. Additionally, third-party libraries and tools, such as

NuGet packages, extend its functionality, making it easier to implement complex features.

- **Type Safety and Strong Typing**: C# is a statically typed language, which means errors can often be caught at compile time rather than runtime. This ensures better reliability and less debugging.

- **Cross-Platform Compatibility**: Traditionally, C# was tied to Windows, but with **.NET Core**, it has become truly cross-platform. .NET Core allows C# applications to run on **Windows, Linux, and macOS**, offering the flexibility to build applications for any major operating system.

- **Integration with Cloud and Mobile**: C# supports integration with cloud services (such as **Microsoft Azure**) and mobile platforms through **Xamarin**. Xamarin enables the creation of mobile apps for iOS, Android, and Windows using a shared codebase in C#.

- **Asynchronous Programming**: C# supports asynchronous programming with features like **async** and **await**, allowing for efficient handling of I/O-bound operations. This is particularly important in cross-platform development, where different systems may have different performance characteristics.

C#'s combination of features makes it a great choice for building scalable, cross-platform applications that can run on multiple devices and environments.

Using .NET Core for Building Cross-Platform Applications

.NET Core is an open-source, cross-platform version of the .NET framework that allows developers to build applications that run on Windows, macOS, and Linux. It brings all the advantages of C# and its ecosystem to a wider range of platforms, making it a key tool for cross-platform development.

Here's how **.NET Core** enhances C# for cross-platform development:

- **Platform Independence**: With .NET Core, you can write a C# application and deploy it on various operating systems without needing to modify the code. This ensures consistency across platforms and reduces development time.
- **Lightweight and Modular**: .NET Core is optimized for performance and has a modular architecture.

29

Developers can choose only the parts of the framework they need, making applications more lightweight and efficient.

- **Unified Development**: .NET Core brings together the best features of different platforms (Windows, Linux, macOS) into a unified development environment. Developers no longer have to worry about platform-specific APIs, making cross-platform development simpler.

- **Command-Line Tools**: .NET Core comes with a powerful set of command-line tools for building, running, and deploying applications. This is particularly useful for developers working in different environments or those looking to automate tasks.

- **Cross-Platform Libraries**: Many libraries, such as **Entity Framework Core** (for database access), **ASP.NET Core** (for web apps), and **Xamarin** (for mobile apps), are designed to work seamlessly across platforms with .NET Core.

Setting Up a C# Development Environment

To start building cross-platform applications with C# using .NET Core, you'll need to set up your development environment. Here's how to do it:

1. **Install .NET SDK**:
   - Go to the official **.NET website** (dotnet.microsoft.com) and download the **.NET SDK** for your operating system (Windows, macOS, or Linux).
   - Follow the installation instructions to complete the setup. After installation, you should be able to run the `dotnet` command from the terminal or command prompt.

2. **Install an Integrated Development Environment (IDE)**:
   - **Visual Studio**: The most popular IDE for C# development is **Visual Studio**, which provides full support for .NET Core and C#. Visual Studio comes with extensive debugging tools, a powerful editor, and integrated tools for building and deploying cross-platform applications.
   - **Visual Studio Code**: For a more lightweight editor, you can use **VS Code**, which, combined with the **C# extension**, provides excellent

support for C# development, including IntelliSense, debugging, and Git integration.

3. **Create a New Project**:

   o Once your environment is set up, you can create a new .NET Core project by running the following command in the terminal:

   ```javascript
   dotnet new console -n
   MyCrossPlatformApp
   ```

   o This command will create a simple console application that you can build and run on any platform. The -n flag specifies the name of your project.

4. **Build and Run the Project**:

   o To build and run the project, navigate to your project folder in the terminal and type:

   ```arduino
   dotnet build
   dotnet run
   ```

   o These commands will compile the project and execute it, allowing you to test your app locally.

5. **Deploy to Multiple Platforms**:

- o With **.NET Core**, once your application is built, you can deploy it to various platforms with little or no modification. Use the command line to package your app and deploy it as needed.

Real-World Example: C# Desktop Application Running on Multiple OS

Let's look at a simple real-world example of building a cross-platform desktop application using **.NET Core** and **Windows Forms** or **WPF (Windows Presentation Foundation)**, though .NET Core supports these with cross-platform capabilities.

Example: Cross-Platform Todo List Application

1. **Step 1: Create a New Windows Forms Application in .NET Core**
    - o In your terminal or command prompt, create a new Windows Forms project:

    ```cpp
    dotnet new winforms -n TodoApp
    ```

    - o This command will set up a basic Windows Forms application.

33

2. **Step 2: Write the Code**

   o Inside the generated `MainForm.cs`, add the necessary components to display a list of tasks and a button to add new tasks. This simple UI includes a **TextBox, Button**, and **ListBox**.

csharp

```csharp
using System;
using System.Windows.Forms;

public class MainForm : Form
{
    private Button addButton;
    private TextBox taskTextBox;
    private ListBox taskListBox;

    public MainForm()
    {
        addButton = new Button { Text = "Add Task", Left = 100, Width = 100, Top = 50 };
        taskTextBox = new TextBox { Left = 100, Width = 200, Top = 20 };
        taskListBox = new ListBox { Left = 100, Width = 200, Height = 200, Top = 80 };

        addButton.Click += (sender, e) =>
        {
```

```
                    if
(!string.IsNullOrEmpty(taskTextBox.Text))
                    {

taskListBox.Items.Add(taskTextBox.Text);
             taskTextBox.Clear();
                    }
            };


            Controls.Add(addButton);
            Controls.Add(taskTextBox);
            Controls.Add(taskListBox);
        }
    }


public static class Program
{
    [STAThread]
    public static void Main()
    {
        Application.EnableVisualStyles();
        Application.Run(new MainForm());
    }
}
```

3. **Step 3: Build and Run the Application**

   o Now that you have the code in place, build and
      run your application using the following
      command:

```
arduino

dotnet build
dotnet run
```

o   This will open a desktop window where you can
    add tasks to a list.

4. **Step 4: Test on Multiple Platforms**

o   Since .NET Core supports cross-platform
    deployment, you can build this application to run
    on macOS or Linux using other UI libraries such
    as **Avalonia** or **GtkSharp** for non-Windows
    systems. Simply modify the UI framework or use
    a cross-platform UI toolkit.

This simple **Todo List application** demonstrates how C#
with .NET Core allows you to build a desktop application
that can run seamlessly across different operating systems,
reducing development time and effort.

CHAPTER 4

GETTING STARTED WITH AGILE DEVELOPMENT

Principles and Practices of Agile Development

Agile development is a set of principles and practices aimed at delivering high-quality software through iterative and incremental development. It focuses on flexibility, collaboration, and customer satisfaction. Here are the key principles of Agile development:

1. **Customer Collaboration Over Contract Negotiation**: Agile emphasizes working closely with the customer or product owner to ensure the product meets their needs, rather than relying solely on contracts and predefined requirements.

2. **Responding to Change Over Following a Plan**: Agile encourages flexibility and adaptation to change. Instead of strictly following an initial plan, Agile teams welcome new requirements, even in late stages of development.

3. **Deliver Working Software Frequently**: Agile promotes delivering small, working increments of

software at regular intervals (usually every 1-2 weeks). This allows teams to gather feedback and improve the product continually.

4. **Individuals and Interactions Over Processes and Tools**: Agile values people and communication over rigid processes and tools. Teams are encouraged to communicate openly and collaborate effectively to solve problems.

5. **Simplicity**: Agile advocates for simplicity in design and functionality. The goal is to deliver the most valuable features with the least complexity.

6. **Self-Organizing Teams**: Agile teams are self-organizing, meaning they have the autonomy to manage their tasks, prioritize work, and make decisions collectively, leading to higher ownership and accountability.

7. **Continuous Improvement**: After each iteration (sprint), teams reflect on their work and identify ways to improve processes and performance.

8. **Face-to-Face Communication**: Although virtual communication is common today, Agile encourages face-to-face interaction for more effective collaboration, as it ensures better understanding and quicker problem resolution.

How Agile Fits Into the Cross-Platform Development Lifecycle

Agile is a perfect fit for cross-platform development, as it promotes flexibility and iterative improvement, which is vital when building applications that must run on multiple operating systems and devices. Here's how Agile aligns with the cross-platform development lifecycle:

- **Frequent Releases**: In cross-platform development, releasing working versions of an app across multiple platforms frequently is crucial. Agile's iterative nature allows for regular updates and releases, ensuring that the app works on all targeted platforms with each new sprint.

- **Testing Across Platforms**: Cross-platform development often involves testing on multiple devices and environments, which can be complex and time-consuming. With Agile, testing is part of every sprint, ensuring that each increment of the software is tested and improved across all platforms regularly.

- **Prioritizing Features**: With Agile, teams work with the product owner to prioritize features based on user needs and business value. For cross-platform applications, this means focusing on core functionalities first, such as syncing data across platforms or ensuring that the UI looks good on all screen sizes, before adding more advanced features.

- **Continuous Feedback**: Agile relies on customer feedback, which is particularly important for cross-platform apps. Users across different platforms (e.g., iOS, Android, Windows, macOS) may have unique preferences and experiences. By incorporating user feedback after each iteration, developers can make improvements and adjust features to cater to different platforms.

- **Adaptation to Changes**: Cross-platform development often involves dealing with new tools, frameworks, or platform-specific requirements that emerge throughout the project. Agile allows teams to quickly adapt to changes, whether they're related to platform updates or changes in the project scope.

Real-World Example: Building Software Iteratively Using Agile

Let's look at a real-world example of how Agile works in the context of cross-platform development. Suppose we are building a **task management application** that needs to run on both mobile (Android and iOS) and desktop (Windows and macOS).

1. **Sprint 1 – Initial Setup and Core Functionality (1-2 weeks)**:

   o **Goal**: Set up the development environment, establish the codebase, and develop the core functionality for adding and managing tasks.

   o **Outcome**:

     ▪ The team creates a basic application structure with the ability to add tasks and view them on mobile devices.

     ▪ The application is only available on one platform for this sprint, but the groundwork for cross-platform compatibility is laid by ensuring the code is modular and platform-independent.

     ▪ During the sprint review, feedback from the stakeholders is gathered, and the team receives input on how to make the app more user-friendly and functional.

2. **Sprint 2 – Cross-Platform Sync and UI (1-2 weeks)**:

   o **Goal**: Implement task synchronization across platforms and enhance the user interface (UI) to make it suitable for mobile and desktop.

   o **Outcome**:

     ▪ The team integrates a cloud service to sync tasks between devices. A user can add a task on their phone, and it will appear on their desktop.

- The team makes sure the UI is responsive and works well on different screen sizes.

- Feedback from stakeholders is collected, focusing on the app's usability and the syncing feature's reliability. Some UI tweaks are requested, and some features are prioritized based on user feedback.

3. **Sprint 3 – Testing, Bug Fixing, and New Features (1-2 weeks)**:

   o **Goal**: Conduct cross-platform testing and fix any bugs related to syncing or UI display. Add new features, such as task categorization or priority setting.

   o **Outcome**:

      - The team runs the app on all supported platforms (iOS, Android, Windows, macOS) and addresses bugs or platform-specific issues, such as resolution problems or performance lags.

      - New features are added, such as the ability to categorize tasks by project or assign priority levels.

- Feedback is gathered again, and the team adjusts features based on real-world usage.

4. **Sprint 4 – Final Testing and Polishing (1-2 weeks)**:

   o **Goal**: Conduct a final round of testing, refine the app, and fix any remaining issues.

   o **Outcome**:

      - The application is now running smoothly across all platforms. The app's design is polished, and all major bugs have been fixed.
      - Stakeholders sign off on the final product.
      - The app is ready for deployment.

Throughout this process, Agile development ensures that the app evolves iteratively, incorporating feedback at each stage. Every sprint results in a functional piece of software that works on multiple platforms and continuously improves based on user needs and platform-specific requirements.

By following Agile principles, the development team avoids the pitfalls of long development cycles and rigid planning, allowing them to stay flexible and deliver a quality product that meets user expectations across multiple platforms.

CHAPTER 5

CREATING CROSS-PLATFORM APPLICATIONS WITH PYTHON

Python Frameworks and Tools for Cross-Platform Development

Python is a highly flexible language, and several frameworks and tools are designed specifically to support cross-platform development. These frameworks help developers build applications that can run on multiple operating systems like Windows, macOS, and Linux, as well as mobile platforms like iOS and Android. Here are a few popular Python frameworks for cross-platform development:

1. **Kivy**:

    o **Kivy** is an open-source Python framework for developing multitouch applications. It's suitable for building both mobile and desktop applications and allows you to write the application once and deploy it on various platforms.

    o **Strengths**: Kivy has built-in support for touch events, multitouch gestures, and accelerometer-based controls, making it a popular choice for developing mobile apps, games, and interactive UIs.

- o **Supported Platforms**: Windows, macOS, Linux, iOS, and Android.

2. **PyQt**:

- o **PyQt** is a set of Python bindings for the Qt application framework, which is widely used for developing desktop applications. It supports creating powerful and professional-looking GUI applications.

- o **Strengths**: PyQt provides tools to create native-looking applications with rich graphical elements and has robust support for event-driven programming.

- o **Supported Platforms**: Windows, macOS, and Linux.

3. **BeeWare**:

- o **BeeWare** is a collection of tools and libraries for building native user interfaces. With BeeWare, you can write applications in Python and deploy them on various platforms without needing to rewrite code.

- o **Strengths**: BeeWare allows you to build apps that feel native to each platform (iOS, Android, Windows, macOS, etc.) and integrates well with native mobile and desktop development environments.

- o **Supported Platforms**: Windows, macOS, Linux, iOS, and Android.

4. **PyGTK**:

- o **PyGTK** is another framework for creating graphical user interfaces, primarily for Linux. It provides a set of Python bindings for the GTK toolkit, which is used in many popular Linux applications.
- o **Strengths**: PyGTK is ideal for developers focusing on Linux but can also be used on other platforms with the proper setup.
- o **Supported Platforms**: Windows, macOS, and Linux.

5. **wxPython**:

- o **wxPython** is a Python wrapper around the wxWidgets C++ toolkit. It's used for creating native desktop applications for Windows, macOS, and Linux.
- o **Strengths**: wxPython provides a native look and feel for applications on each platform.
- o **Supported Platforms**: Windows, macOS, and Linux.

These frameworks provide the essential tools for developing cross-platform applications, each with its strengths depending on the type of application you want to build (e.g., mobile, desktop, or game apps).

Example of Building a Simple GUI Application

Let's create a simple **To-Do List** application with a basic graphical user interface (GUI) using **Kivy**. This example will help you understand how to use Kivy to build cross-platform applications. We'll build an app that allows users to add tasks to a list.

1. **Install Kivy**: First, install Kivy using pip:

```nginx
pip install kivy
```

2. **Write the Application Code**:

Here's the code for a simple to-do list application:

```python
from kivy.app import App
from kivy.uix.boxlayout import BoxLayout
from kivy.uix.textinput import TextInput
```

```
from kivy.uix.button import Button
from kivy.uix.label import Label

class TodoApp(App):
    def build(self):
        self.tasks = []

        # Create the main layout
        layout                                  =
BoxLayout(orientation='vertical',    padding=10,
spacing=10)

        # Create the input field
        self.input_task                         =
TextInput(hint_text="Enter       a       task",
size_hint_y=None, height=40)
        layout.add_widget(self.input_task)

        # Create the add task button
        add_button   =   Button(text="Add   Task",
size_hint_y=None, height=50)
        add_button.bind(on_press=self.add_task)
        layout.add_widget(add_button)

        # Create a label to display tasks
        self.task_list                          =
BoxLayout(orientation='vertical',
size_hint_y=None)
        layout.add_widget(self.task_list)
```

```
        return layout

    def add_task(self, instance):
        task = self.input_task.text.strip()
        if task:
            self.tasks.append(task)
            self.update_task_list()
        self.input_task.text = ""   # Clear the
input field

    def update_task_list(self):
        self.task_list.clear_widgets()
        for task in self.tasks:

self.task_list.add_widget(Label(text=task,
size_hint_y=None, height=40))

if __name__ == '__main__':
    TodoApp().run()
```

Explanation of the code:

- **BoxLayout**: A layout container that arranges widgets vertically or horizontally. In this example, it's used for both the main layout and the task list.
- **TextInput**: A widget for entering text (used for typing tasks).
- **Button**: A button that users can click to add tasks.

- **Label**: A widget for displaying text. Here, it's used to display the tasks in the to-do list.

3. **Run the Application**: After writing the code, you can run it by executing the script:

```nginx
```

```
python todo_app.py
```

This will open a window with a text input, a button, and a list to display tasks. Users can add tasks, and they will be displayed in the list.

Deploying the Application Across Different Operating Systems

To deploy this application across different operating systems, Kivy provides tools to package and distribute your app as standalone executables. Here's how you can do it:

1. **Windows**:
   o Use **PyInstaller** or **cx_Freeze** to create a Windows executable.
   o Install PyInstaller using pip:

```nginx
```

```
pip install pyinstaller
```

- o To create an executable:

```css
```

```
pyinstaller --onefile todo_app.py
```

- o This will generate a `todo_app.exe` file that can be distributed on Windows systems.

2. **macOS**:
    - o Kivy applications can be packaged for macOS using **py2app**.
    - o Install py2app:

```nginx
```

```
pip install py2app
```

    - o Create a `setup.py` script and use py2app to build the app for macOS.

3. **Linux**:
    - o On Linux, Kivy apps are often packaged using **PyInstaller** (similar to Windows).
    - o Install PyInstaller:

```nginx
```

```
pip install pyinstaller
```

- o Package the app as an executable using the same command:

```
css
```

```
pyinstaller --onefile todo_app.py
```

4. **Mobile (Android & iOS)**:
   - o For mobile platforms like Android and iOS, you can use **Buildozer** for packaging the application. Buildozer automates the process of creating Android (APK) or iOS (IPA) packages.
   - o Install Buildozer:

```
nginx
```

```
pip install buildozer
```

   - o Then, configure Buildozer and run:

```
nginx
```

```
buildozer android debug
```

This process will generate a native package for your targeted platform. Once the application is packaged, you can distribute it through app stores (like Google Play or the App

Store for mobile apps) or share the executables for desktop platforms.

By using Kivy, you can easily create a simple Python app that works across different platforms, and with the help of tools like PyInstaller, py2app, or Buildozer, you can deploy your application seamlessly to various devices and operating systems.

CHAPTER 6

DEVELOPING CROSS-PLATFORM APPLICATIONS WITH C# AND .NET CORE

Introduction to .NET Core and Xamarin for Cross-Platform Apps

.NET Core is a free, open-source, and cross-platform framework developed by Microsoft for building modern, cloud-based, and internet-connected applications. It enables developers to create applications that run on **Windows**, **macOS**, and **Linux**, making it an ideal solution for building cross-platform apps using **C#**.

Here's why **.NET Core** is a strong choice for cross-platform development:

- **Performance**: .NET Core is designed to be lightweight, modular, and optimized for performance, which makes it well-suited for cross-platform applications, from mobile apps to web and microservices.
- **Unified Platform**: .NET Core unifies the development of backend services and frontend applications. Developers can write server-side code in C# for APIs, databases, and

microservices, while the same C# skills can be applied to mobile and desktop apps.

- **Active Community and Microsoft Support**: With backing from Microsoft and a vibrant open-source community, .NET Core continues to evolve with regular updates, new features, and a broad ecosystem of libraries and tools.

Xamarin is a cross-platform mobile development framework that extends the .NET Core ecosystem to the world of mobile apps. Xamarin allows developers to use **C#** and **.NET Core** to build **native mobile applications** for **iOS**, **Android**, and **Windows** from a single codebase. Xamarin abstracts the platform-specific differences, making it easier to maintain cross-platform apps.

- **Xamarin.Forms**: This allows developers to create UIs that can be shared across platforms, while still accessing native device APIs.
- **Xamarin.Native**: Developers can use Xamarin.Native if they need to build platform-specific UIs while still sharing the same backend code.

Using **.NET Core** and **Xamarin**, developers can create high-performance, native-like apps for multiple platforms using the same C# codebase, reducing development time and ensuring consistency across platforms.

Creating and Deploying Apps with C#

The process of building and deploying a cross-platform app with **C#** using **.NET Core** and **Xamarin** involves the following steps:

1. **Set Up the Development Environment**:
    - Install **Visual Studio** (recommended IDE for C# development). Visual Studio provides full support for both **.NET Core** and **Xamarin**.
        - Visual Studio can be downloaded from Microsoft's website.
        - Ensure to install the necessary workloads for **.NET Core** and **Xamarin** during the installation process.

2. **Create a New Xamarin Project**:
    - Open Visual Studio and create a new Xamarin.Forms project.
    - Choose **File → New Project**, and select the **Xamarin.Forms App** template under **Mobile**.
    - Visual Studio will generate the basic structure for your Xamarin application, including platform-

specific folders for **iOS**, **Android**, and **UWP** (**Universal Windows Platform**).

3. **Develop the App**:

   o Write the app's business logic and functionality using C# in the shared project. Xamarin provides a simple way to share code across all platforms by defining the business logic in the shared **Portable Class Library (PCL)** or **.NET Standard** library.

   o Use **Xamarin.Forms** to build the user interface in XAML (markup language), which will render appropriately on all platforms. Example of a simple **Xamarin.Forms** code snippet for creating a button:

```csharp
public class MainPage : ContentPage
{
    public MainPage()
    {
        Button button = new Button
        {
            Text = "Click Me!"
        };

        button.Clicked += (sender,
args) =>
```

```
        {
            DisplayAlert("Button
Clicked", "You clicked the button",
"OK");
        };

        Content = new StackLayout
        {
            Children = { button }
        };
    }
}
```

4. **Test the Application**:

   o Xamarin provides built-in emulators for testing your app on various devices (Android, iOS, and Windows). Alternatively, you can also use physical devices for testing.

   o Use the **Xamarin Live Player** or **Visual Studio Emulator** to test the app on different platforms to ensure that it works seamlessly.

5. **Package the App**:

   o After testing and refining the app, you can build and package the app for deployment.

     ▪ For **Android**, you will create an APK file by building the app with Xamarin's tools.

- For **iOS**, you can build an IPA file and submit it to the **Apple App Store** using **Xcode**.
- For **Windows**, you can package the app as an MSIX package and submit it to the **Microsoft Store**.

6. **Deploy the App**:

   o Once packaged, the app can be deployed to app stores (Google Play Store, Apple App Store, Microsoft Store) or distributed privately.

   o To deploy the app to Google Play or Apple App Store, you'll need to create developer accounts with each platform (Google Developer Console for Android and Apple Developer Program for iOS).

   o For **Windows**, you can deploy the app directly to the Windows Store or distribute it via internal networks.

Real-World Example: Building a Cross-Platform Mobile App

Let's walk through building a simple **To-Do List App** with **Xamarin.Forms** that runs on Android and iOS.

1. **Create a New Xamarin Project**:

   o Open **Visual Studio** and create a **Xamarin.Forms App** project.

59

o Choose a **Blank App** template to get started with a clean slate.

2. **Design the UI**:

o In the shared project's **MainPage.xaml** file, define the layout for the to-do list:

```xml
xml

<?xml version="1.0" encoding="utf-8"
?>
<ContentPage
xmlns="http://xamarin.com/schemas/2
014/forms"

xmlns:x="http://schemas.microsoft.c
om/winfx/2006/xaml"

x:Class="TodoApp.MainPage">

    <StackLayout Padding="20">
        <Entry    x:Name="TaskEntry"
Placeholder="Enter task here" />
        <Button    Text="Add    Task"
Clicked="OnAddTaskClicked" />
        <ListView
x:Name="TaskListView" />
    </StackLayout>
</ContentPage>
```

3. **Handle Button Click and Add Task**:

    o   In the **MainPage.xaml.cs** file, add the logic for adding tasks to a list:

```csharp
public partial class MainPage :
ContentPage
{
    List<string> tasks = new
List<string>();

    public MainPage()
    {
        InitializeComponent();
    }

    async                        void
OnAddTaskClicked(object        sender,
EventArgs e)
    {
        if
(!string.IsNullOrWhiteSpace(TaskEnt
ry.Text))
        {

tasks.Add(TaskEntry.Text);

TaskListView.ItemsSource = null;
```

```
TaskListView.ItemsSource = tasks;
        TaskEntry.Text        =
string.Empty;
            }
        }
    }
```

4. **Test the Application**:
    o   Test the app on both **Android** and **iOS** emulators using Visual Studio.
    o   Ensure that tasks are added to the list when the user types and clicks the button.

5. **Build and Deploy**:
    o   Build the app for both **Android** and **iOS**.
    o   Use **Xamarin's tools** to generate APK and IPA files for Android and iOS respectively.
    o   Deploy the APK to the **Google Play Store** and the IPA to the **Apple App Store**.

Conclusion

With **.NET Core** and **Xamarin**, you can create fully functional, high-performance mobile applications that run across **iOS**, **Android**, and **Windows**. By using a single **C#** codebase and leveraging Xamarin's cross-platform capabilities, you can streamline development and maintain consistent functionality across all platforms. This makes it easier to focus on creating great user experiences without needing to manage multiple codebases for each platform.

CHAPTER 7

CLOUD INTEGRATION: WHY AND HOW TO USE CLOUD SERVICES IN DEVELOPMENT

Benefits of Integrating Cloud Services (AWS, Azure, Google Cloud)

Integrating **cloud services** into your development process brings a host of benefits that can streamline your development workflow, improve scalability, and increase the overall reliability of your applications. Major cloud providers such as **Amazon Web Services (AWS)**, **Microsoft Azure**, and **Google Cloud** offer a wide range of services that make it easier to develop, deploy, and maintain applications. Here are some of the key benefits of using cloud services:

1. **Scalability**:
   o Cloud platforms offer **elasticity**, allowing applications to scale up or down based on demand. For example, AWS provides auto-scaling features that automatically adjust the number of servers to handle increased traffic.

- o Whether you're building a web app, mobile app, or enterprise solution, the cloud can handle varying workloads without the need for expensive infrastructure investments.

2. **Cost Efficiency**:
   - o Cloud services operate on a **pay-as-you-go** model, meaning you only pay for the resources you use. This model helps developers avoid upfront costs and allows businesses to scale costs according to usage.
   - o You don't need to manage your own data centers, servers, or hardware, reducing the total cost of ownership.

3. **High Availability and Reliability**:
   - o Leading cloud providers offer services designed to be highly available and fault-tolerant. **AWS** and **Azure** provide global data centers that ensure your application remains up and running even if a server or region fails.
   - o Features like **load balancing** and **failover** ensure that traffic is efficiently managed, and resources are distributed to prevent downtime.

4. **Security**:
   - o Cloud providers have extensive security measures in place, such as **encryption**, **firewalls**,

and **multi-factor authentication**, to safeguard sensitive data.

- o AWS, Azure, and Google Cloud all offer security services like **Identity and Access Management (IAM)**, which helps control who can access specific resources.

5. **Global Reach**:

- o Cloud services have a global network of servers, allowing you to serve users in multiple regions around the world with minimal latency.
- o You can deploy applications in multiple geographic locations, ensuring faster performance for users regardless of their location.

6. **Managed Services**:

- o Cloud providers offer managed services that take care of the administrative overhead, such as database management, backups, and monitoring. This frees up developers to focus on writing code rather than managing infrastructure.

7. **Integration with Development Tools**:

- o Cloud platforms integrate seamlessly with various development tools and CI/CD pipelines, streamlining the software development lifecycle.
- o AWS offers **AWS CodePipeline**, **Azure DevOps**, and **Google Cloud Build** for continuous integration and deployment, making it

easier to automate workflows and deliver updates more efficiently.

Cloud Computing Fundamentals and How to Choose the Right Provider

Cloud Computing refers to the delivery of computing services like servers, storage, databases, networking, software, and more over the internet. There are three primary types of cloud computing models:

1. **Infrastructure as a Service (IaaS)**:
   - ○ This is the most fundamental cloud service model, offering virtualized computing resources over the internet. IaaS provides the basic building blocks for cloud infrastructure, such as virtual machines, networking, and storage. Providers like **AWS EC2** and **Azure Virtual Machines** are IaaS services.

2. **Platform as a Service (PaaS)**:
   - ○ PaaS provides a platform that allows developers to build, deploy, and manage applications without worrying about the underlying infrastructure. Popular PaaS offerings include **AWS Elastic Beanstalk**, **Google App Engine**, and **Azure App Services**.

3. **Software as a Service (SaaS)**:
   o SaaS delivers software applications over the internet on a subscription basis. Examples include **Google Workspace** (formerly G Suite), **Microsoft Office 365**, and **Salesforce**. While SaaS isn't directly used for development, it offers cloud-based software solutions that developers can integrate into their applications.

When choosing a cloud provider, consider the following factors:

- **Use Case and Services**: Different cloud providers excel in different areas. **AWS** has a vast range of services, making it ideal for complex or enterprise-level applications. **Google Cloud** is highly regarded for big data, machine learning, and Kubernetes support. **Azure** is often favored by businesses that already use Microsoft tools and services.

- **Pricing Model**: Compare pricing across the cloud providers to ensure that you get the most cost-effective solution. Each provider offers a free tier with limited resources for developers to test their services.

- **Support and Ecosystem**: Consider the level of customer support and the community around the cloud platform. AWS, Azure, and Google Cloud all provide documentation, customer support, and a developer ecosystem to help with troubleshooting and integration.

- **Security and Compliance**: Check the security measures offered by each provider, especially if you're dealing with sensitive data. Ensure that the provider meets industry-specific compliance standards like **GDPR**, **HIPAA**, or **SOC 2**.

- **Performance and Availability**: Consider the data center locations of each provider. Choose a provider with data centers close to your target users to minimize latency.

Real-World Example: Building a Cloud-Connected Application

Let's build a simple cloud-connected **To-Do List Application** that stores user tasks in the cloud and allows users to access them from any device. For this example, we'll use **AWS** to store the tasks in a cloud database, using **AWS DynamoDB**, and we'll connect the app using **AWS SDK for .NET**.

1. **Set Up AWS DynamoDB**:
   - First, sign up for an AWS account if you don't have one.
   - Navigate to the **DynamoDB** section in the AWS Management Console.
   - Create a new table called `ToDoTasks` with `TaskId` as the primary key.

2. **Create a .NET Core Application**:
   - Open **Visual Studio** and create a new **ASP.NET Core Web API** project.
   - Install the **AWSSDK.DynamoDBv2** NuGet package to interact with DynamoDB:

   ```mathematica
   Install-Package AWSSDK.DynamoDBv2
   ```

3. **Configure AWS SDK**:
   - Set up your AWS credentials by creating an **IAM user** with access to DynamoDB and configure the AWS SDK to use these credentials.
   - In your `appsettings.json`, add the AWS region:

   ```json
   {
       "AWS": {
   ```

70

```
                    "Region": "us-west-2"
                }
            }
```

4. **Build the API to Interact with DynamoDB**:

      o   In your API controller, create methods to add and retrieve tasks from DynamoDB.

csharp

```csharp
using Amazon.DynamoDBv2;
using Amazon.DynamoDBv2.DocumentModel;
using Microsoft.AspNetCore.Mvc;

[ApiController]
[Route("[controller]")]
public class TodoController : ControllerBase
{
    private    readonly    AmazonDynamoDBClient
_dynamoDbClient;
    private    readonly    string    _tableName    =
"ToDoTasks";

    public    TodoController(AmazonDynamoDBClient
dynamoDbClient)
    {
        _dynamoDbClient = dynamoDbClient;
    }
```

```
[HttpPost]
public     async     Task<IActionResult>
AddTask(string task)
    {
        var              table              =
Table.LoadTable(_dynamoDbClient, _tableName);
        var taskDocument = new Document();
        taskDocument["TaskId"]              =
Guid.NewGuid().ToString();
        taskDocument["Task"] = task;

        await table.PutItemAsync(taskDocument);
        return Ok("Task added successfully");
    }


    [HttpGet]
    public async Task<IActionResult> GetTasks()
    {
        var              table              =
Table.LoadTable(_dynamoDbClient, _tableName);
        var     search     =     table.Scan(new
ScanFilter());
        var     tasks     =     await
search.GetRemainingAsync();

        return Ok(tasks);
    }
}
```

5. **Deploy the Application**:

- Once your API is built, deploy it using **AWS Elastic Beanstalk** or any other hosting solution. Elastic Beanstalk simplifies deployment by automatically managing the infrastructure for your app.

6. **Access Data from the Cloud**:
   - Once the application is running, you can add tasks via a POST request and retrieve them with a GET request. The data is stored in **DynamoDB** and can be accessed globally, from any device.

By using AWS, we've made the To-Do List app cloud-connected, allowing users to store and retrieve tasks from anywhere. The cloud setup provides scalability and reliability, ensuring that even as the app grows, it remains responsive and stable.

This example highlights how cloud services like AWS can be used to handle backend infrastructure, making it easier for developers to build and deploy cloud-connected applications. The integration of cloud databases like DynamoDB, along with the simplicity of cloud services, makes building robust, scalable applications easier than ever.

CHAPTER 8

LEVERAGING CLOUD STORAGE FOR CROSS-PLATFORM APPLICATIONS

Using Cloud Storage Services Like AWS S3, Azure Blob Storage

Cloud storage services like **AWS S3 (Simple Storage Service)** and **Azure Blob Storage** allow developers to store large amounts of data, including user files, images, and documents, in the cloud. These services are designed to handle vast quantities of unstructured data, making them ideal for cross-platform applications that need to store and manage user data across multiple devices and platforms.

1. **AWS S3 (Simple Storage Service)**:
   o **AWS S3** is one of the most popular cloud storage services. It allows you to store and retrieve any amount of data at any time from anywhere on the web. S3 is commonly used to store static assets like images, videos, and backups for cross-platform apps.
   o **Benefits**:

- **Scalability**: S3 scales automatically to meet the needs of your app, whether you're storing a few files or millions of them.
- **High Availability**: S3 provides high durability (99.999999999% durability) and availability.
- **Cost-Effective**: With AWS's pay-as-you-go pricing model, you only pay for what you use.
- **Security**: S3 offers robust security features, such as encryption, access control, and identity management.

2. **Azure Blob Storage**:
   - **Azure Blob Storage** is a service provided by Microsoft for storing large amounts of unstructured data, such as text and binary data, including documents, images, and videos. It's designed to work seamlessly with Azure's other services.
   - **Benefits**:
     - **Integration with Azure**: Easy integration with other Azure services like Azure Functions, Azure Logic Apps, and Azure Cognitive Services.

- **Access Control**: Fine-grained access control with Azure's role-based access control (RBAC) and shared access signatures (SAS).
- **Scalability**: Just like AWS S3, Azure Blob Storage automatically scales to meet your needs.
- **Global Distribution**: With Azure's global presence, you can store data in data centers around the world, ensuring low-latency access for users.

Both AWS S3 and Azure Blob Storage are essential tools for handling large amounts of unstructured data, enabling cross-platform apps to seamlessly manage files and other media. They can be used to store and retrieve content such as user-generated media (photos, videos), application logs, or any other data that needs to be shared across devices.

Managing User Data and Media Across Platforms

Managing user data and media across multiple platforms is one of the primary challenges in cross-platform app development. Cloud storage services like AWS S3 and Azure Blob Storage provide an easy and secure way to store and access this data consistently across different platforms (iOS, Android, Windows, and macOS). Here's how cloud storage can streamline this process:

1. **Unified Data Access**:
   o By storing user data and media in the cloud, developers can ensure that the data is accessible from any device, at any time, and from anywhere. For example, a user can upload an image from their mobile device, and that image will be available on their desktop application in real-time, without the need for synchronization logic.

2. **Automatic Sync Across Devices**:
   o Cloud storage solutions allow data to be automatically synced across devices. For example, if a user uploads a file (e.g., an image or document) from a mobile app, the file can be accessed through a desktop app or another mobile device. The cloud acts as a central repository where the data is always up-to-date across platforms.

3. **Handling Media Files**:
   o Media files such as photos, videos, and audio files often require special handling to ensure that they are stored efficiently and retrieved quickly. Cloud storage solutions like S3 and Azure Blob Storage offer powerful features like **content delivery**

networks **(CDNs)** and **caching** to ensure that media files are delivered to users with low latency, regardless of their location.

4. **Managing Large Files**:

    o   With large media files, such as high-definition videos or large documents, cloud storage services provide automatic scalability and ensure that file sizes do not overwhelm local device storage. Cloud services also offer direct upload and download capabilities, ensuring the process is optimized for each platform.

5. **Data Security and Backup**:

    o   Both AWS S3 and Azure Blob Storage offer strong data protection features, such as **encryption at rest** and **SSL/TLS encryption during transfer**, ensuring that user data is secure. Additionally, cloud providers handle regular backups, so you don't need to worry about data loss due to device failures or outages.

Real-World Example: Syncing App Data Across Devices Using Cloud Storage

Let's consider a real-world scenario where we are building a **cross-platform photo-sharing app**. The app will allow users to upload images, view them across different devices, and share them with friends. Here's how we can integrate **AWS S3** for seamless syncing of media data across platforms.

1. **Set Up AWS S3**:
    - First, we need to create an AWS S3 bucket where we will store the images.
        - Log into your **AWS Console** and navigate to **S3**.
        - Create a new bucket called `photo-sharing-app-images`.
        - Set the bucket to be private, ensuring that only authenticated users can upload or access files.

2. **App Development for iOS and Android (Cross-Platform)**:
    - We'll use **Xamarin.Forms** to develop a cross-platform mobile app for **iOS** and **Android**. The app will allow users to upload images to the cloud and display images from the cloud.
    - **Install AWS SDK**: In your Xamarin project, install the **AWSSDK.S3** NuGet package to enable S3 interaction.

    ```mathematica
    Install-Package AWSSDK.S3
    ```

3. **Upload Image to S3**:

   o The following code snippet shows how you can upload an image from a mobile app to **AWS S3**:

```csharp
using Amazon.S3;
using Amazon.S3.Model;

public async Task UploadImageToS3(string
imagePath)
{
    var s3Client = new
AmazonS3Client(Amazon.RegionEndpoint.USEa
st1);
    var putRequest = new PutObjectRequest
    {
        BucketName = "photo-sharing-app-
images",
        Key = Path.GetFileName(imagePath),
        FilePath = imagePath,
        ContentType = "image/jpeg"
    };
    await
s3Client.PutObjectAsync(putRequest);
}
```

4. **Sync Data Across Devices**:

- o Once the image is uploaded to S3, it can be accessed from any device. To retrieve the image on another device, you can use the `GetObjectRequest` method:

```csharp
public async Task<string>
GetImageUrlFromS3(string imageName)
{
    var s3Client = new
AmazonS3Client(Amazon.RegionEndpoint.USEa
st1);
    var getRequest = new GetObjectRequest
    {
        BucketName = "photo-sharing-app-
images",
        Key = imageName
    };
    var response = await
s3Client.GetObjectAsync(getRequest);
    return response.HttpStatusCode ==
HttpStatusCode.OK ?
response.ResponseUri.ToString() : null;
}
```

5. **Display Image on Different Devices**:
   - o After the image is uploaded to S3, the app can display the image by fetching the URL returned

by the `GetImageUrlFromS3` method. This ensures that the image is available across both mobile and desktop apps, synced in real-time via the cloud.

o For example, you can use the **ImageView** component in Xamarin.Forms to show the image from the URL:

```csharp
var imageUrl = await GetImageUrlFromS3("image_name.jpg");
imageView.Source = ImageSource.FromUri(new Uri(imageUrl));
```

6. **Managing User Data (Text, Comments, etc.)**:

o Along with media files, user-generated content such as text, comments, and metadata (e.g., image description) can be stored in **AWS DynamoDB** or **Azure Cosmos DB** to handle relational data. This allows you to sync user comments and metadata across devices in real-time.

By leveraging **AWS S3** for storing images and syncing them across devices, the app ensures that users can access their photos from any device, whether they are on mobile, tablet, or desktop. The use of cloud storage makes managing media files efficient, scalable, and secure.

Conclusion

Cloud storage services like **AWS S3** and **Azure Blob Storage** play a crucial role in enabling cross-platform applications to store and sync user data, media, and other files. By using these services, you can easily manage large media files, ensure seamless syncing across devices, and offer a smooth, reliable user experience. Additionally, cloud storage solutions provide scalability, security, and global accessibility, making them essential for building modern cross-platform apps.

CHAPTER 9

INTEGRATING PYTHON AND C# IN A SINGLE APPLICATION

How Python and C# Can Work Together in One Application

Integrating **Python** and **C#** in a single application allows developers to leverage the strengths of both languages. Python is known for its simplicity, flexibility, and large ecosystem of libraries, while C# excels in performance, robustness, and the ability to build cross-platform applications using .NET Core and Xamarin.

There are several ways that Python and C# can work together in one application:

1. **Backend in Python, Frontend in C#:**
    - Python can be used for tasks like data processing, machine learning, or interacting with external APIs, while C# handles the frontend or the user interface.
    - Python's ease of use in handling complex algorithms and its large selection of data science libraries makes it ideal for backend tasks, while C# can handle the performance-intensive aspects

of the UI, such as drawing graphics or managing user interactions.

2. **API-Based Communication**:

   o One of the most common ways to integrate Python and C# is by using an **API** to communicate between the two. Python can serve as a backend that exposes RESTful APIs (using frameworks like Flask or FastAPI), while C# can make requests to these APIs and display the results in the frontend.

3. **Interfacing Python with C# Using Libraries**:

   o Another approach is using libraries that allow direct interfacing between Python and C#. For instance:

      ▪ **Python for .NET (pythonnet)**: This library allows you to call .NET libraries directly from Python. It provides a seamless way to interoperate between Python and C#.

      ▪ **IronPython**: This is an implementation of Python that runs on the .NET framework, allowing you to run Python code directly within a C# application.

4. **Shared File Formats (e.g., JSON, CSV)**:

   o Python and C# can communicate by reading and writing shared file formats. For example, Python can write data to a JSON file, and C# can read that file and use the data in the frontend. This approach is useful for exchanging structured data.

Interfacing Python with C# Using APIs or Other Techniques

There are a few methods that you can use to allow Python and C# to communicate with each other efficiently. Here's how to approach it:

1. **Using REST APIs**:
   - One of the most efficient ways to interface Python with C# is through RESTful APIs. Python can be used to build a backend service using web frameworks like **Flask** or **FastAPI**. The Python backend can expose endpoints that C# can call via HTTP requests.

   Example:

   - Python Backend (Flask API):

   ```python
   from flask import Flask, jsonify

   app = Flask(__name__)
   ```

```python
@app.route('/api/data')
def get_data():
    return        jsonify({"message":
"Hello from Python!"})


if __name__ == '__main__':
    app.run(debug=True)
```

- o **C# Frontend (Using** `HttpClient`**):**

csharp

```csharp
using System;
using System.Net.Http;
using System.Threading.Tasks;

class Program
{
    static async Task Main(string[]
args)
    {
        HttpClient   client   =   new
HttpClient();
        HttpResponseMessage response
=                        await
client.GetAsync("http://localhost:5
000/api/data");

        if
(response.IsSuccessStatusCode)
```

```
        {
                string    data    =    await
response.Content.ReadAsStringAsync(
);

Console.WriteLine($"Response        from
Python: {data}");
        }
    }
}
```

2. **Using Python for .NET (pythonnet)**:

   o **pythonnet** allows Python to call C# code directly. This is useful when you need to run Python code inside a .NET application or access .NET libraries from Python.

   To use pythonnet:

   o Install the library via `pip`:

   ```
   nginx
   ```

   ```
   pip install pythonnet
   ```

   o You can then import .NET namespaces and classes directly into your Python code:

   ```
   python
   ```

```
import clr
clr.AddReference('System.Windows.Fo
rms')
from    System.Windows.Forms    import
MessageBox

MessageBox.Show("Hello   from   Python
with C#!")
```

3. **Using IronPython**:

   o **IronPython** is an implementation of Python running on the .NET framework. It allows you to run Python scripts directly within a C# application. You can embed Python scripts in your C# project and call Python functions as needed.

Example:

   o C# with embedded IronPython:

```csharp
csharp

using IronPython.Hosting;
using Microsoft.Scripting.Hosting;

class Program
{
```

```
static void Main(string[] args)
{
        ScriptEngine    engine    =
Python.CreateEngine();

engine.Execute("print('Hello     from
Python in C#')");
    }
}
```

4. **Using Shared File Formats**:
   o Python and C# can also communicate by sharing data in a common file format, such as **JSON**, **XML**, or **CSV**.
     - Python can write data to a file (e.g., JSON) that C# can read and process.
     - C# can then write output to a file that Python can process, allowing the two programs to communicate without direct interaction.

Example:

   o Python writing JSON:

```python

import json
```

```python
data  =  {"message":  "Hello  from
Python"}
with open('data.json', 'w') as f:
    json.dump(data, f)
```

o **C# reading JSON:**

```csharp
csharp

using System;
using System.IO;
using Newtonsoft.Json;

class Program
{
    static void Main(string[] args)
    {
        string        json        =
File.ReadAllText("data.json");
        var        data        =
JsonConvert.DeserializeObject<dynam
ic>(json);
        Console.WriteLine($"Message
from Python: {data.message}");
    }
}
```

Real-World Example: A Python Backend with a C# Frontend

Let's walk through a real-world example where **Python** handles the backend logic (e.g., data processing, machine learning model execution) and **C#** is used for the frontend (e.g., user interface). We'll use **Flask** for the Python backend and a **C#** console app to interact with the backend.

1. **Python Backend (Flask API)**:
   - Python will handle processing and expose an API endpoint that returns results.

```python
python

from flask import Flask, jsonify
import math

app = Flask(__name__)

@app.route('/api/square/<int:number>')
def get_square(number):
    result = math.pow(number, 2)
    return jsonify({"number": number,
"square": result})

if __name__ == '__main__':
    app.run(debug=True)
```

The Flask API will calculate the square of a number sent as a URL parameter and return the result as a JSON response.

2. **C# Frontend (Console Application)**:
   - The C# application will make HTTP requests to the Flask API, retrieve the data, and display it to the user.

```csharp
using System;
using System.Net.Http;
using System.Threading.Tasks;
using Newtonsoft.Json.Linq;

class Program
{
    static async Task Main(string[] args)
    {
        Console.WriteLine("Enter a number to get its square:");
        int number = Convert.ToInt32(Console.ReadLine());

        HttpClient client = new HttpClient();
        HttpResponseMessage response = await
```

```
client.GetAsync($"http://localhost:5000/a
pi/square/{number}");

        if (response.IsSuccessStatusCode)
        {
            string     data     =     await
response.Content.ReadAsStringAsync();
            JObject          json          =
JObject.Parse(data);
            Console.WriteLine($"The square
of {json["number"]} is {json["square"]}");
        }
        else
        {
            Console.WriteLine("Error:
Unable   to   retrieve   data   from   the
backend.");
        }
    }
}
```

In this scenario, the C# console app interacts with the Python backend, sends a request to calculate the square of a number, and prints the result.

Conclusion

Integrating **Python** and **C#** in a single application allows developers to utilize the strengths of both languages. Python

94

can be used for tasks like data processing, machine learning, or server-side logic, while C# handles the frontend or user interface. Using methods like **REST APIs**, **pythonnet**, **IronPython**, and shared file formats, Python and C# can work together seamlessly in a cross-platform environment. The real-world example of a Python backend and C# frontend shows how this integration can create powerful, flexible applications for a wide range of use cases.

CHAPTER 10

VERSION CONTROL WITH GIT: ESSENTIAL FOR COLLABORATIVE DEVELOPMENT

The Importance of Git in Team-Based Development

Git is a distributed version control system (VCS) that allows teams to track changes in their codebase, collaborate effectively, and maintain a history of the project's evolution. Git is a crucial tool for **team-based development** for several reasons:

1. **Collaboration**:
   o Git allows multiple developers to work on the same project simultaneously, making it easy to collaborate and merge changes without conflicts. Developers can work on their local copies of the code and then sync their changes to a central repository, which ensures that the entire team is working on the most up-to-date version of the code.

2. **Branching and Merging**:

   o Git's **branching** feature allows developers to work on features, bug fixes, or experiments without affecting the main codebase (usually called the **master** or **main** branch). Once a feature is complete, it can be merged back into the main branch after review.

   o This workflow helps teams to develop and test new features independently while keeping the main codebase stable.

3. **Tracking Changes**:

   o Git provides a detailed history of all changes made to the codebase. Each change is logged with metadata, including the developer's name, date, and description. This makes it easy to trace bugs or issues back to specific changes in the code, facilitating better debugging and collaboration.

4. **Code Review**:

   o Git enables a structured **code review process** through pull requests. Developers can submit their changes for review, allowing team members to evaluate the code before it's merged into the main branch. This ensures that the code meets quality standards and is reviewed by others.

5. **Backup and Recovery**:

- o Git provides a distributed nature, meaning that every developer's local repository contains a full history of the project. If something goes wrong, you can always revert to a previous version of the code or recover lost work by referencing past commits.

6. **Conflict Resolution**:
   - o In team environments, conflicts are inevitable when multiple people work on the same part of the code. Git helps identify these conflicts and allows developers to resolve them manually. It also helps in keeping a clean, understandable history of how the conflicts were resolved.

How to Set Up Git for Managing Code Across Multiple Platforms

Setting up Git for a project involves configuring a local Git repository, connecting to a remote repository (e.g., on GitHub, GitLab, or Bitbucket), and managing code across multiple platforms. Here's how to get started:

1. **Install Git**:
   - o First, install Git on your machine. You can download it from git-scm.com.
   - o After installation, you can verify that Git is set up by running the following command in your terminal or command prompt:

```
css
```

```
git --version
```

2. **Set Up Global Configuration**:

   o After installing Git, set up your global configuration with your name and email. This information will be associated with your commits.

   ```
   bash
   ```

   ```
   git config --global user.name "Your
   Name"
   git config --global user.email
   "youremail@example.com"
   ```

3. **Create a Local Repository**:

   o To start versioning your project with Git, navigate to the root directory of your project and run the following command to initialize a Git repository:

   ```
   bash
   ```

   ```
   git init
   ```

4. **Add Files to the Repository**:

o   To track files in your repository, use the `git add` command:

```bash
```

```bash
git add .
```

This command stages all changes in the project directory. To stage specific files, replace the dot (`.`) with the file name.

5. **Commit Changes**:

o   After staging the changes, commit them to the local repository with a descriptive message:

```bash
```

```bash
git commit -m "Initial commit"
```

6. **Set Up a Remote Repository**:

o   Create a repository on a Git hosting platform like **GitHub**, **GitLab**, or **Bitbucket**.

o   To link the local repository to the remote one, use the following command:

```bash
```

```
git      remote      add      origin
https://github.com/username/reposit
ory.git
```

7. **Push Changes to the Remote Repository**:

- o After committing changes locally, push them to the remote repository:

```
bash
```

```
git push -u origin master
```

8. **Cloning a Repository on Another Platform**:

- o If you're working across multiple platforms (e.g., developing on both Windows and macOS), you can **clone** the repository to another machine by using:

```
bash
```

```
git                               clone
https://github.com/username/reposit
ory.git
```

- o This ensures that your codebase is synchronized between platforms.

Real-World Example: Git Workflow for a Cross-Platform Project

Let's walk through a real-world example of how **Git** is used in a typical workflow for a **cross-platform project**. In this case, we'll assume that the project is a **cross-platform mobile app** built with **Xamarin** (C#) and a **Python backend**.

1. **Initial Setup**:
   o The team begins by setting up a **Git repository** on **GitHub** for the mobile app project. The repository contains two main directories: one for the **Xamarin frontend** and one for the **Python backend**.
   o The project is initialized by one team member using:

   bash

   ```
   git init
   git        remote        add        origin
   https://github.com/team/project.git
   ```

2. **Creating and Working with Branches**:

o   Each developer works on a specific feature, and they create their own branch to work independently:

```bash
```

```bash
git checkout -b feature/login-page
```

o   On this branch, the developer works on the login page for the mobile app (in Xamarin). They commit changes as they go:

```bash
```

```bash
git add .
git commit -m "Added login page UI"
```

3. **Merging Changes**:

o   Once the feature is complete, the developer pushes their branch to the remote repository:

```bash
```

```bash
git push origin feature/login-page
```

o   The developer then opens a **pull request** on GitHub, where the team can review the code.

After the code is reviewed and approved, it is merged into the **main** branch:

```bash
git checkout main
git pull origin main
git merge feature/login-page
git push origin main
```

4. **Syncing with the Python Backend**:

    o Meanwhile, another developer is working on the **Python backend**. They set up a separate branch for their work:

    ```bash
    git checkout -b feature/user-authentication
    ```

    o After working on the authentication endpoints in the backend, they commit their changes and push them:

    ```bash
    git add .
    ```

```
git    commit    -m    "Added    user
authentication API"
git    push    origin    feature/user-
authentication
```

5. **Testing and Collaboration**:

   o Both developers now test the integration between the frontend (Xamarin) and the backend (Python). The mobile app interacts with the backend API to authenticate users.

   o They ensure that the **frontend** is properly calling the **Python API**, and everything works as expected.

6. **Final Merging and Deployment**:

   o Once all features are complete, the code is merged into the **main** branch, and the final version is tagged for deployment:

   ```bash

   git tag v1.0
   git push origin v1.0
   ```

   o The team now deploys the **backend** to the cloud (AWS or Azure), and the **mobile app** is deployed to the **Google Play Store** and **Apple App Store**.

105

7. **Collaborative Development with Multiple Platforms**:

   o   As development continues, developers use **Git** to ensure that their changes are synchronized across different platforms (e.g., Windows for C# and macOS for Python). This allows them to ensure that the project runs smoothly on all platforms while maintaining a single source of truth in the remote repository.

Conclusion

Git is an essential tool for managing code in team-based development, especially in cross-platform projects. It provides an effective way to collaborate, track changes, manage branches, and ensure that code is synchronized across different platforms. By following Git workflows like **branching**, **merging**, and **pull requests**, teams can work efficiently and minimize conflicts. Whether you're working on a mobile app with a Python backend or any other cross-platform project, Git ensures that collaboration remains smooth and organized.

CHAPTER 11

AGILE METHODOLOGY IN PRACTICE: ITERATIVE DEVELOPMENT AND CONTINUOUS IMPROVEMENT

How to Implement Agile in Cross-Platform Development

Agile methodology is ideal for **cross-platform development** because it emphasizes flexibility, quick iteration, and continuous feedback, which are essential when developing apps for different platforms (e.g., iOS, Android, Windows, macOS). Implementing Agile in cross-platform development focuses on delivering working software incrementally, adjusting to changing requirements, and ensuring high-quality results at each stage.

Here's how you can implement Agile effectively in cross-platform development:

1. **Sprint-Based Development**:
   - Agile divides development into short cycles known as **sprints**, typically lasting 1-4 weeks.

Each sprint focuses on delivering a small, manageable feature or enhancement. For cross-platform apps, this might include developing a new feature that works across all platforms (iOS, Android, and web) within a single sprint.

- o At the beginning of each sprint, the team decides on specific cross-platform features to prioritize and deliver, such as implementing a feature on both the mobile and desktop versions of the app.

2. **Cross-Platform Collaboration**:

- o Agile emphasizes team collaboration, so cross-functional teams (including designers, developers, testers, and product owners) work together from the start to ensure alignment on the project's goals.
- o This collaboration is key when managing multiple platforms to ensure that a feature is consistently implemented and tested across all platforms, even if platform-specific adjustments are needed.

3. **Frequent Feedback**:

- o Agile's focus on frequent feedback ensures that cross-platform developers can quickly identify and address issues, ensuring that features work consistently across platforms.

- o Regular reviews and demos allow stakeholders to see working features after each sprint, providing feedback that can be incorporated into the next iteration.

4. **Integration and Testing**:
   - o In cross-platform development, integrating code for multiple platforms can be challenging. Agile methodologies encourage frequent integration of code (e.g., at the end of each sprint) to ensure that features are consistently tested and integrated across all platforms.
   - o Automated tests are often used to ensure the app's functionality works consistently across devices, reducing the risk of bugs or platform-specific issues.

5. **User Stories and Prioritization**:
   - o **User stories** are used to break down features into smaller, manageable tasks that are easier to implement within a sprint. In cross-platform development, user stories can be written in a way that considers the requirements for all platforms.
   - o The product backlog is prioritized based on business value, and features that are important for all platforms (e.g., login functionality, synchronization across devices) are often prioritized early on.

Using Scrum and Kanban for Project Management

In Agile, **Scrum** and **Kanban** are two common methodologies used for managing workflows. Both can be applied to cross-platform development, depending on the team's needs.

1. **Scrum**:
    - Scrum is an Agile framework that uses **sprints** to deliver incremental updates. Scrum teams typically consist of a **Product Owner**, **Scrum Master**, and **Development Team**.
    - Scrum works well in cross-platform development because it provides a structured framework to manage multiple tasks while ensuring all stakeholders are aligned on goals and progress.
    - The Scrum workflow typically includes:
        - **Product Backlog**: A prioritized list of features and tasks.
        - **Sprint Planning**: A meeting where the team selects which tasks (user stories) to work on during the sprint.
        - **Daily Standups**: Short meetings to discuss progress, roadblocks, and next steps.

110

- **Sprint Review**: A demonstration of the features completed during the sprint.

- **Sprint Retrospective**: A meeting for the team to reflect on the sprint and suggest improvements.

2. **Kanban**:

   o Kanban is another Agile methodology that focuses on continuous delivery without strict timeboxes. Kanban uses a visual **board** with columns representing the various stages of work (e.g., "To Do," "In Progress," and "Done").

   o In cross-platform development, Kanban helps teams visualize the flow of tasks, ensuring that features for different platforms move through development stages at an appropriate pace.

   o Kanban focuses on:

      - **Work In Progress (WIP) Limits**: Restricting the number of tasks in any given stage to improve focus and efficiency.

      - **Continuous Delivery**: Delivering small improvements or features on a regular basis, instead of waiting for a full sprint to complete.

Real-World Example: Agile Sprints in Developing Cross-Platform Software

Let's walk through an example of how **Agile sprints** are used in developing a **cross-platform task management application** with a backend written in **Python** and a frontend in **Xamarin (C#)** for both Android and iOS.

1. **Sprint 1 – Setup and Core Features (1-2 weeks)**:
   - **Goal**: Set up the project environment, create a basic user interface, and integrate core functionality (e.g., task creation, user login).
   - **User Stories**:
     - As a user, I want to create a new task, so I can manage my to-do list.
     - As a user, I want to sign in to the app with my credentials, so I can sync my tasks across devices.
   - **Tasks**:
     - Set up Xamarin project for Android and iOS.
     - Implement user authentication using a Python-based backend API.
     - Create a basic UI for task creation and display.
   - **End of Sprint Review**:

- The development team demonstrates the basic task creation feature on both Android and iOS.
- Product Owner and stakeholders review the feature and suggest improvements.

2. **Sprint 2 – Syncing and Additional Features (2 weeks)**:
   - **Goal**: Implement task synchronization between Android, iOS, and the Python backend.
   - **User Stories**:
     - As a user, I want my tasks to sync across devices, so I can access my tasks from both my phone and tablet.
     - As a user, I want to mark tasks as completed, so I can track my progress.
   - **Tasks**:
     - Implement API calls to sync tasks between the mobile apps and backend (using Python).
     - Add "mark task as completed" functionality.
     - Test syncing functionality across Android and iOS platforms.
   - **End of Sprint Review**:

- The team demonstrates the task sync feature, where tasks marked as completed on one platform are reflected on the other platform.
- Feedback is gathered to address UI issues and performance improvements.

3. **Sprint 3 – Testing, Bug Fixes, and Polish (2 weeks)**:

   o **Goal**: Perform cross-platform testing and fix bugs related to task synchronization and user experience.

   o **User Stories**:

      - As a user, I want to experience seamless task synchronization between platforms without any delays or data loss.
      - As a user, I want the app's performance to be optimal, even when I have a large number of tasks.

   o **Tasks**:

      - Conduct manual testing on Android and iOS.
      - Identify and fix any bugs related to syncing and task management.
      - Optimize performance by addressing issues with large task lists.

   o **End of Sprint Review**:

- The team presents the app with improved performance and bug fixes. Stakeholders review the performance improvements and confirm that the app is now ready for production.

4. **Sprint 4 – Final Touches and Deployment (1-2 weeks)**:

   o **Goal**: Prepare the app for production deployment, including final UI adjustments and preparing the app for submission to the App Store and Google Play.

   o **User Stories**:
      - As a user, I want the app to have a clean, intuitive interface, so I can easily navigate through tasks.
      - As a user, I want to receive notifications when a task is due, so I can stay on track.

   o **Tasks**:
      - Final UI tweaks based on feedback from previous sprints.
      - Integrate push notifications for task reminders.
      - Prepare app for submission to App Store and Google Play.

   o **End of Sprint Review**:

- The team demonstrates the final version of the app, including task reminders and polished UI.
- The app is deployed to both app stores.

Conclusion

Implementing **Agile methodology** in cross-platform development enables teams to work efficiently, adapt to changing requirements, and continuously improve their product. By breaking down work into manageable **sprints**, using **Scrum** or **Kanban** for project management, and prioritizing collaboration and feedback, teams can deliver high-quality features across multiple platforms. The real-world example of developing a cross-platform task management app illustrates how Agile sprints can be applied to handle both frontend (Xamarin) and backend (Python) development while maintaining a strong focus on iterative improvement.

CHAPTER 12

ENSURING CODE QUALITY AND TESTABILITY IN CROSS-PLATFORM PROJECTS

Techniques for Writing Maintainable and Testable Code

Writing maintainable and testable code is essential in cross-platform development to ensure that your application remains scalable, bug-free, and easy to update over time. Here are some key techniques for writing high-quality code:

1. **Follow Coding Standards**:
   - Establish consistent **coding standards** for the entire team, such as naming conventions, indentation, and commenting practices. This ensures that the codebase is clean, easy to understand, and easy to collaborate on.
   - Use tools like **linters** (e.g., **Pylint** for Python, **StyleCop** for C#) to enforce coding standards automatically.

2. **Separation of Concerns**:
   - Ensure that each module or class has a single responsibility and doesn't handle unrelated tasks.

117

For example, separate business logic, UI components, and data handling.

- o Use design patterns like **MVC (Model-View-Controller)** or **MVVM (Model-View-ViewModel)** to structure your code in a way that makes it easy to update and maintain.

3. **Write Modular Code**:

- o Break your application into smaller, reusable components. Modular code is easier to maintain, test, and extend.

- o Use **dependency injection** where possible to decouple components and make it easier to replace or mock dependencies for testing.

4. **Use Comments and Documentation**:

- o While code should be self-explanatory, comments are helpful for complex logic. Make sure to add clear comments that explain the purpose and behavior of critical sections of code.

- o **Automated documentation tools** like **Swagger** for APIs or **Sphinx** for Python can help generate up-to-date documentation directly from your code.

5. **Refactor Regularly**:

- o Over time, as your project grows, parts of your code may become difficult to maintain or extend.

Refactor code regularly to improve readability and maintainability.

- o **Code reviews** are a valuable tool in identifying areas of the code that can be refactored or optimized.

6. **Implement Error Handling**:

- o Use robust error handling mechanisms to deal with unexpected issues gracefully. This includes proper exception handling in both Python and C#.
- o Implement logging to capture runtime errors and provide useful insights during debugging.

Automated Testing Strategies for Python and C#

Automated testing ensures that your application behaves as expected and reduces the risk of bugs when making changes or adding new features. Here are common automated testing strategies for **Python** and **C#**:

1. **Unit Testing**:

- o **Unit testing** focuses on testing small, isolated units of code (e.g., functions or methods). It helps ensure that individual components work correctly and allows you to catch errors early.
- o In **Python**, you can use **unittest** or **pytest** for unit testing.

o In **C#**, you can use **NUnit** or **xUnit** for writing unit tests.

2. **Integration Testing**:

o Integration tests verify that different components of your application work together as expected. In cross-platform development, this may include testing interactions between the mobile app and the backend.

o In **Python**, you can use **pytest** with **fixtures** to set up and tear down integrations.

o In **C#**, integration tests can be written using **xUnit** or **NUnit** with a focus on database or API integration.

3. **UI Testing**:

o UI tests ensure that the user interface functions correctly. For cross-platform mobile apps, this includes verifying that buttons, forms, and other UI elements behave as expected across devices.

o In **Python**, **Selenium** can be used for web UI testing, while **Appium** is an option for mobile app testing.

o In **C#**, **Appium** or **Xamarin.UITest** can be used for automated UI testing of mobile apps.

4. **Continuous Integration (CI) and Continuous Deployment (CD)**:

      o   Implementing **CI/CD pipelines** ensures that your tests run automatically when code is committed to the repository. Services like **Jenkins, Travis CI**, and **GitHub Actions** can automate running tests and deploying code.

      o   CI/CD pipelines are crucial for cross-platform development to ensure consistent behavior across all platforms after every change.

5. **Test Coverage**:

      o   **Test coverage** tools help ensure that your code is well-tested. These tools measure which parts of your code have been executed by tests and highlight areas that may require more testing.

      o   In **Python**, tools like **coverage.py** provide code coverage reports.

      o   In **C#**, **Visual Studio** provides built-in test coverage tools that work with unit tests.

Real-World Example: Unit Testing in Both Python and C#

Let's walk through a real-world example of unit testing in both **Python** and **C#** for a simple **task management application** that has functionality for adding and completing tasks. The application has a backend in **Python** and a frontend in **C# (Xamarin)**.

1. **Python: Unit Testing the Task Management API**

Let's say you have a Python-based API that provides functionality for adding tasks. You want to write unit tests to ensure the task creation function works correctly.

- **Python Code (Task API)**:

python

```
class TaskManager:
    def __init__(self):
        self.tasks = []

    def add_task(self, task):
        if not task:
            raise ValueError("Task cannot
be empty")
        self.tasks.append(task)
        return task

# Sample usage:
task_manager = TaskManager()
task_manager.add_task("Complete        the
project")
```

- **Unit Test for the TaskManager**:

python

```
import unittest
```

```python
from task_manager import TaskManager

class TestTaskManager(unittest.TestCase):
    def setUp(self):
        self.task_manager = TaskManager()

    def test_add_task(self):
        task = "Complete the project"
        result                          =
self.task_manager.add_task(task)
        self.assertEqual(result, task)
        self.assertIn(task,
self.task_manager.tasks)

    def test_add_empty_task(self):
        with
self.assertRaises(ValueError):

self.task_manager.add_task("")

if __name__ == '__main__':
    unittest.main()
```

- **Explanation**:
    - o `test_add_task`: Tests that a task is correctly added to the `TaskManager`.
    - o `test_add_empty_task`: Ensures that adding an empty task raises a `ValueError`.

2. **C#: Unit Testing the TaskManager in Xamarin**

Let's assume the C# Xamarin frontend needs to interact with the **TaskManager** API. You want to write unit tests for the C# part of the code that interacts with the backend.

- **C# Code (TaskManager)**:

```csharp
public class TaskManager
{
    private List<string> tasks = new
List<string>();

    public string AddTask(string task)
    {
        if
(string.IsNullOrWhiteSpace(task))
        {
            throw                    new
ArgumentException("Task cannot be empty");
        }
        tasks.Add(task);
        return task;
    }

    public IEnumerable<string> GetTasks()
=> tasks;
```

```
}
```

- **Unit Test for TaskManager in C#:**

```
csharp


using NUnit.Framework;
using System;

[TestFixture]
public class TestTaskManager
{
    private TaskManager taskManager;

    [SetUp]
    public void Setup()
    {
        taskManager = new TaskManager();
    }

    [Test]
    public void TestAddTask()
    {
        string task = "Complete the
project";
        string           result           =
taskManager.AddTask(task);
        Assert.AreEqual(task, result);
    }
```

```
[Test]
public void TestAddEmptyTask()
{
```

```
Assert.Throws<ArgumentException>(()        =>
taskManager.AddTask(""));
    }
}
```

- **Explanation**:
  - `TestAddTask`: Verifies that a task is added correctly to the `TaskManager`.
  - `TestAddEmptyTask`: Ensures that an empty task raises an `ArgumentException`.

3. **Running the Tests**:
   - In **Python,** you can run the tests using:

   ```bash
   ```

   ```
   python          -m          unittest
   test_task_manager.py
   ```

   - In **C#,** you can run the tests using the **Test Explorer** in **Visual Studio** or using the **dotnet test** command:

   ```bash
   ```

```
dotnet test
```

Conclusion

Ensuring **code quality** and **testability** is essential in cross-platform development to create maintainable, bug-free applications. Techniques like following **coding standards**, **modular code**, and **separation of concerns** improve the maintainability of your project, while **automated testing** ensures that your app works correctly across different platforms. The real-world examples of **unit testing in Python** and **C#** demonstrate how you can ensure functionality for both backend and frontend code, ultimately helping you deliver a reliable, scalable cross-platform app.

CHAPTER 13

OPTIMIZING PERFORMANCE IN CROSS-PLATFORM APPLICATIONS

Performance Challenges and Solutions for Cross-Platform Development

Cross-platform development provides great flexibility, but it also comes with performance challenges. While developers can create a single codebase for multiple platforms (e.g., iOS, Android, Windows), these platforms often have different performance characteristics, hardware, and software environments. Optimizing performance across all platforms can be tricky. Here are some common challenges and solutions for cross-platform development:

1. **Platform-Specific Performance Bottlenecks**:
   o Each platform has its own set of APIs, libraries, and resources that may not be optimized in the same way. For example, what works well on iOS might not be as efficient on Android or Windows.
   o **Solution**: Use platform-specific optimizations when necessary, while maintaining a unified

codebase. For example, use conditional compilation or platform-specific code to address performance bottlenecks for specific platforms.

2. **Memory Management**:

   o Cross-platform apps, especially those with complex features, can consume a significant amount of memory. Managing memory across multiple platforms is challenging, as different platforms may handle memory allocation and garbage collection differently.

   o **Solution**: Use memory profiling tools to track and optimize memory usage. Minimize memory usage by optimizing data structures and caching mechanisms.

3. **UI Rendering and Responsiveness**:

   o In cross-platform apps, rendering the user interface (UI) in a way that performs well on all devices can be challenging. Differences in screen size, resolution, and GPU power can affect rendering performance.

   o **Solution**: Use **Lazy Loading**, **Image Compression**, and **GPU Rendering** to optimize UI performance. Make sure to only load UI elements when they are visible on the screen to save processing time and memory.

4. **Background Processes**:

- o Cross-platform apps may have background processes, such as fetching data, synchronizing with cloud services, or updating notifications. These processes can slow down the app if not optimized.
- o **Solution**: Offload heavy tasks to background threads or services. Use **asynchronous programming** (like Python's `asyncio` or C#'s `async` and `await`) to ensure that these processes don't block the main UI thread.

5. **Network Performance**:
   - o Many cross-platform apps rely on network requests to fetch data from cloud services or interact with APIs. Slow or inefficient network communication can degrade the user experience.
   - o **Solution**: Optimize network requests by reducing the number of API calls, caching responses, and using **compressed data formats** (e.g., JSON or Protobuf) to minimize data transfer sizes.

Tools and Techniques for Profiling and Optimizing Code

To address the performance challenges in cross-platform development, it is important to use profiling and optimization tools to identify bottlenecks and improve performance. Below are some key tools and techniques for profiling and optimizing code in both **Python** and **C#**:

1. **Profiling Tools**:
   - **Python**:
     - **cProfile**: A built-in Python module that helps profile your code, allowing you to track time spent on different functions and methods.

       ```python
       import cProfile
       cProfile.run('your_function()
       ')
       ```

     - **line_profiler**: A third-party tool that provides line-by-line profiling to help you understand how much time each line of your code takes.
     - **memory_profiler**: A tool to profile memory usage in Python applications, which helps detect memory leaks and areas of high memory consumption.
     - **Py-Spy**: A sampling profiler that works in real-time, which can be used to profile

long-running Python processes with minimal overhead.

- o **C#:**

  - ▪ **Visual Studio Profiler**: Visual Studio provides built-in profiling tools that can analyze CPU usage, memory consumption, and performance bottlenecks.

  - ▪ **dotTrace**: A powerful tool for profiling .NET applications, helping to find bottlenecks in CPU, memory, and threading performance.

  - ▪ **BenchmarkDotNet**: A popular library for benchmarking and performance testing in .NET applications.

  - ▪ **CLR Profiler**: This tool can help analyze memory usage and garbage collection in .NET applications.

2. **Code Optimization Techniques**:

   - o **Minimize Expensive Operations**: Identify and optimize slow operations like loops, recursion, or API calls that are executed frequently.

   - o **Use Asynchronous Code**: For non-blocking operations (e.g., API calls, file I/O), use asynchronous techniques like Python's `asyncio` or C#'s `async/await` to keep the UI responsive and reduce the risk of slow performance.

- o **Optimize Data Structures**: Choose the appropriate data structures (e.g., dictionaries, sets, lists) for the task at hand. Avoid unnecessary large data structures, as they can impact both memory usage and speed.

- o **Use Efficient Algorithms**: Make sure that the algorithms you're using are optimal for the size and complexity of the data they operate on. Use **Big O** notation to evaluate the efficiency of your code.

3. **Memory Management**:

- o **Garbage Collection**: Both Python and C# have automatic garbage collection, but you can optimize memory usage by manually managing resources when needed. In Python, be mindful of **circular references** and **large object graphs**, while in C#, ensure objects are disposed of properly.

- o **Caching**: Use in-memory caching to store frequently used data, reducing the need to repeatedly fetch or compute the same data. Libraries like **functools.lru_cache** in Python and **MemoryCache** in C# can help implement caching mechanisms.

4. **Network Optimization**:

  o **Reduce API Calls**: Implement **batching** and **pagination** to reduce the number of API requests needed. If possible, combine multiple requests into a single API call to reduce overhead.

  o **Compression**: Use data compression (e.g., **gzip**) to reduce the size of network responses, speeding up data transfer.

  o **Timeouts and Retries**: Implement retry logic and set reasonable timeouts for network requests to avoid blocking the app during slow or unreliable network conditions.

Real-World Example: Optimizing a Python App for Mobile Platforms

Let's consider a **Python backend** for a **mobile app** that fetches and processes large amounts of user data. The backend is hosted on a cloud server, and the mobile app needs to access this data quickly to provide a smooth user experience. Here's how we can optimize the Python app for mobile platforms:

1. **Problem**: The app is experiencing slow performance when fetching user data from the cloud. The mobile

app waits for a long time before receiving the response, resulting in a poor user experience.

2. **Profiling**:
   - First, use the **cProfile** module to identify performance bottlenecks in the Python app.

```python
import cProfile
from myapp import fetch_data_from_database

cProfile.run('fetch_data_from_database()'
)
```

   - After profiling, we notice that the database queries are slow and take a significant amount of time to process.

3. **Optimization**:
   - **Database Indexing**: Improve query performance by adding proper indexes to frequently accessed columns in the database.
   - **Caching**: Implement a caching mechanism using **Redis** to cache frequently requested data and avoid repeated database queries.

```python
import redis
```

```
r    =    redis.StrictRedis(host='localhost',
port=6379, db=0)
cached_data = r.get('user_data')
if cached_data is None:
    user_data = fetch_data_from_database()
    r.set('user_data', user_data, ex=300)
# Cache data for 5 minutes
else:
    user_data = cached_data
```

- o **Asynchronous Requests**: Use **asyncio** to handle multiple API requests asynchronously, preventing the backend from blocking while waiting for database queries to complete.

python

```
import asyncio
import aiohttp

async def fetch_user_data(user_id):
    async with aiohttp.ClientSession() as
session:
        async                        with
session.get(f'https://api.example.com/use
r/{user_id}') as response:
            return await response.json()
```

```
async def main():
    users = [1, 2, 3]
    tasks = [fetch_user_data(user_id) for
user_id in users]
    return await asyncio.gather(*tasks)

asyncio.run(main())
```

4. **Compression**:

   o **Compress Responses**: Use **gzip** compression to minimize the data size for each network response from the server.

```python
import gzip

def compress_response(data):
    return gzip.compress(data.encode('utf-
8'))
```

5. **Testing and Deployment**:

   o After optimizing the app, test it thoroughly by running it under different network conditions (e.g., slow network, high latency) to ensure that it performs well across mobile devices.

o   Deploy the updated backend and ensure that the mobile app connects to the optimized backend, providing a smoother user experience.

Conclusion

Optimizing performance in cross-platform applications involves addressing challenges related to platform-specific issues, memory management, UI responsiveness, and network performance. Using profiling tools and applying techniques like **asynchronous programming**, **caching**, and **compression** can significantly improve the performance of both the frontend and backend. In the real-world example of optimizing a **Python app for mobile platforms**, the combination of database optimizations, asynchronous requests, and data compression helped reduce response times, improving the overall user experience. These techniques can be adapted and applied to various cross-platform projects to ensure efficient, high-performance applications.

CHAPTER 14

SECURITY CONSIDERATIONS IN CROSS-PLATFORM DEVELOPMENT

Common Security Risks in Cross-Platform Applications

Cross-platform applications, while offering the benefit of a unified codebase across multiple platforms, can introduce specific security challenges. Here are some common security risks to be aware of:

1. **Insecure Data Storage**:
   - Storing sensitive data, such as user credentials or personal information, insecurely on devices can lead to data breaches if the device is compromised. This is especially risky in mobile apps, where physical access to the device can be a threat.
   - **Solution**: Use **encryption** to securely store sensitive data. For mobile apps, use platform-specific secure storage solutions, like **Keychain (iOS)** or **Keystore (Android)**. For web-based

apps, use **secure cookies** or **localStorage** with encryption.

2. Weak Authentication:

o If your authentication system is weak, attackers could bypass login mechanisms and gain unauthorized access to user accounts. This is a major concern for cross-platform apps that may rely on both native and web-based authentication methods.

o **Solution**: Use strong, multi-factor authentication (MFA) and ensure that password policies enforce the use of strong passwords (e.g., minimum length, complexity). Implement session expiration and token-based authentication (like JWT) for web and mobile apps.

3. Insecure API Communication:

o Cross-platform apps often communicate with backend services through APIs. If APIs are not properly secured, attackers could intercept and manipulate sensitive data transmitted over the network, exposing vulnerabilities.

o **Solution**: Always use **HTTPS** (SSL/TLS) to encrypt API communication. Additionally, implement API authentication mechanisms (e.g., **OAuth**, **API keys**) to ensure only authorized users can access certain endpoints.

4. **Cross-Site Scripting (XSS)**:
   o XSS attacks involve injecting malicious scripts into web pages viewed by users, which can lead to session hijacking, data theft, or spreading malware.
   o **Solution**: Sanitize and validate all input from users, including form fields and URL parameters, to prevent malicious code from being executed in the browser.

5. **Cross-Site Request Forgery (CSRF)**:
   o CSRF attacks occur when a malicious website sends unauthorized requests on behalf of an authenticated user without their consent. This is particularly concerning in web-based cross-platform apps.
   o **Solution**: Use anti-CSRF tokens to verify that the request was initiated by the intended user. Additionally, ensure that sensitive actions require re-authentication or confirmation from the user.

6. **Insufficient Session Management**:
   o Weak session management can allow attackers to hijack user sessions or exploit vulnerabilities in session handling, especially in cross-platform apps that run on different devices.
   o **Solution**: Use **secure, HttpOnly, SameSite cookies** for session management. Implement

proper session expiration, invalidate sessions after logout, and store minimal session data on the client-side.

How to Secure Your Code and Protect User Data

Securing your code and protecting user data in cross-platform development requires implementing best practices and adopting appropriate security measures. Here's how to do it:

1. **Code Obfuscation**:
   - Obfuscating your code makes it harder for attackers to reverse-engineer your app and extract sensitive information.
   - Use tools like **Dotfuscator** for C# or **pyarmor** for Python to obfuscate the source code and make reverse engineering more difficult.

2. **Encrypt Sensitive Data**:
   - Encrypt sensitive data both at rest (on the device or server) and in transit (when being sent over the network).
   - For mobile apps, use **AES (Advanced Encryption Standard)** for encryption and **SSL/TLS** for securing API communication. For web applications, use **HTTPS** and ensure

sensitive data, such as passwords, is hashed using a secure algorithm (e.g., **bcrypt**, **Argon2**).

3. **Secure Authentication**:

   o   Use secure methods for user authentication. **OAuth** and **OpenID Connect** are popular protocols for enabling secure access to user accounts, especially when integrating third-party services (e.g., Google, Facebook).

   o   Always use **strong passwords** (e.g., requiring a combination of uppercase, lowercase, numbers, and special characters), and consider implementing **multi-factor authentication (MFA)** to add an extra layer of protection.

4. **Validate and Sanitize Input**:

   o   Always validate user input on both the client and server sides. This prevents common injection attacks like **SQL injection**, **XSS**, and **command injection**.

   o   Use libraries or built-in functions for input sanitization and validation. For example, use **OWASP's ESAPI** (Enterprise Security API) for common security tasks in Java or Python.

5. **Secure APIs**:

   o   Implement proper authentication and authorization for your APIs to ensure only authorized users can access them. **OAuth 2.0** or

JWT (JSON Web Tokens) are popular standards for API authentication.

- o Rate-limit API requests to prevent abuse and implement logging to monitor suspicious activity.
- o Ensure APIs follow the **principle of least privilege**, giving users and services access only to the data and functions they need.

6. **Use Secure Dependencies**:

- o Ensure that all third-party libraries or SDKs you use are up to date and have no known vulnerabilities.
- o Use tools like **Dependabot** (GitHub) or **Snyk** to automatically check for vulnerabilities in your dependencies.

7. **Regular Security Audits**:

- o Perform regular security audits on your application to identify and fix potential vulnerabilities. You can use tools like **OWASP ZAP** or **Burp Suite** to scan your application for common security issues.

Real-World Example: Secure Login for a Cross-Platform App Using Cloud Authentication

Let's walk through an example of **securing the login process** for a cross-platform app using **cloud**

authentication. We'll use **Firebase Authentication** for a simple and secure login system that works across both **Android** and **iOS**.

1. **Set Up Firebase Authentication**:
   - First, sign up for a Firebase account and create a new project at Firebase Console.
   - Enable **Email/Password Authentication** or **OAuth** (e.g., Google, Facebook) in the Firebase Authentication settings.

2. **Integrating Firebase Authentication in Xamarin (C#)**:
   - Add the **Firebase SDK** to your Xamarin project using **NuGet**. Install the `Xamarin.Firebase.Auth` package.
   - Configure Firebase in your app by adding the necessary credentials and setting up the Firebase connection in the `MainActivity.cs` (for Android) or `AppDelegate.cs` (for iOS).

3. **Implement Secure Login in Xamarin**:
   - Use Firebase Authentication to securely sign in users. Here's a simple example of how to implement email/password login in Xamarin:

```
csharp
```

```
using Firebase.Auth;
using System;
using Xamarin.Forms;

public class LoginPage : ContentPage
{
    private Entry emailEntry;
    private Entry passwordEntry;

    public LoginPage()
    {
        emailEntry   =   new   Entry   {
Placeholder = "Email" };
        passwordEntry   =   new   Entry   {
Placeholder = "Password", IsPassword = true
};

        var loginButton = new Button
        {
            Text = "Login"
        };
        loginButton.Clicked              +=
OnLoginClicked;

        Content = new StackLayout
        {
            Children   =   {   emailEntry,
passwordEntry, loginButton }
        };
```

```
    }

    private          async          void
OnLoginClicked(object sender, EventArgs e)
    {
        try
        {
            var        authProvider      =
FirebaseAuth.Instance;
            var      user      =      await
authProvider.SignInWithEmailAndPasswordAs
ync(emailEntry.Text, passwordEntry.Text);
            // Successful login - navigate
to the main app page
            await Navigation.PushAsync(new
MainPage());
        }
        catch (Exception ex)
        {
            // Handle login error
            await    DisplayAlert("Error",
ex.Message, "OK");
        }
    }
}
```

4. **Secure the Data**:

   o Firebase Authentication automatically secures
      user credentials by using **SSL/TLS** for all

communications between the client app and the Firebase server.

- o For additional security, implement **MFA (Multi-Factor Authentication)** to require users to provide a second form of verification (e.g., a text message with a one-time code) in addition to their password.

5. **Session Management**:

- o Firebase handles user session management automatically. Once a user logs in, Firebase stores the session token and automatically maintains the session until the user logs out.
- o You can check the authentication state with:

```csharp

if (FirebaseAuth.Instance.CurrentUser !=
null)
{
    // User is logged in
}
else
{
    // User is not logged in
}
```

6. **Logout**:

- o To securely log users out, simply call:

148

```csharp

FirebaseAuth.Instance.SignOut();
```

7. **Testing and Deployment**:
   o Ensure that you test your login system on both Android and iOS platforms, verifying that user credentials are securely authenticated and that the session is maintained across devices.

Conclusion

Ensuring the security of cross-platform applications requires a comprehensive approach, addressing common security risks like insecure data storage, weak authentication, and insecure API communication. By implementing strong security practices such as **encrypted data storage**, **multi-factor authentication**, and **secure API communication**, you can safeguard user data and improve the trustworthiness of your application. In the real-world example of **secure login** using **Firebase Authentication**, the integration of cloud authentication provides a simple yet powerful way to secure user login across multiple platforms.

CHAPTER 15

HANDLING DATABASES IN CROSS-PLATFORM APPLICATIONS

Choosing the Right Database for Your Cross-Platform App (SQL vs. NoSQL)

When building cross-platform applications, one of the most important decisions you'll make is choosing the right database to store and manage your data. **SQL** and **NoSQL** databases each have their strengths and weaknesses, and the choice between them depends on the type of data, scalability needs, and the application's structure. Here's an overview of both:

1. **SQL Databases**:
   o **Relational databases** (SQL) store data in tables with predefined schemas. These databases are ideal for applications with structured data that requires complex queries, relationships between tables, and data integrity.

- o Popular SQL databases include **MySQL, PostgreSQL, Microsoft SQL Server**, and **SQLite**.
- o **Advantages**:
  - **ACID Compliance**: SQL databases offer strong consistency guarantees and support **ACID** (Atomicity, Consistency, Isolation, Durability) properties.
  - **Complex Queries**: SQL supports complex joins, transactions, and other advanced querying features.
  - **Data Integrity**: SQL databases are excellent for maintaining data integrity with constraints and relationships.
- o **Use Cases**: Applications with complex relationships, e-commerce, banking systems, and applications that require high levels of consistency and data integrity.

2. **NoSQL Databases**:
- o **NoSQL** databases are non-relational and store data in various formats, such as documents, key-value pairs, graphs, or wide-column stores. These databases are ideal for applications that need to scale horizontally and handle large volumes of unstructured or semi-structured data.

- o Popular NoSQL databases include **MongoDB, Cassandra, Firebase Realtime Database**, and **Amazon DynamoDB**.
- o **Advantages**:
    - **Scalability**: NoSQL databases are designed for horizontal scaling, which makes them ideal for handling large volumes of data across distributed systems.
    - **Flexible Schema**: NoSQL databases do not require a fixed schema, allowing you to store unstructured or semi-structured data (e.g., JSON, XML).
    - **High Availability**: Many NoSQL databases offer built-in replication and failover capabilities for high availability.
- o **Use Cases**: Real-time applications, social media platforms, big data, IoT applications, and apps with rapidly changing data or where the schema is not well-defined.

Connecting to Databases from Python and C#

Connecting to databases from your cross-platform application depends on the language and database you are using. Here's how you can connect to both **SQL** and **NoSQL** databases in **Python** and **C#**:

1. **Connecting to SQL Databases in Python**:
   - o For **SQL databases** like **MySQL** or **PostgreSQL**, Python offers libraries like **MySQL Connector** or **psycopg2** for PostgreSQL to facilitate connections.

Example of connecting to **MySQL**:

```python
import mysql.connector

# Establish a connection
conn = mysql.connector.connect(
    host="your_host",
    user="your_user",
    password="your_password",
    database="your_database"
)

# Create a cursor to interact with the
database
cursor = conn.cursor()

# Execute a query
cursor.execute("SELECT * FROM tasks")

# Fetch results
tasks = cursor.fetchall()
```

```
for task in tasks:
    print(task)


# Close the connection
cursor.close()
conn.close()
```

2. **Connecting to NoSQL Databases in Python**:
   - For **NoSQL databases** like **MongoDB**, Python offers the **PyMongo** library for easy interaction.

   Example of connecting to **MongoDB**:

```python
python

from pymongo import MongoClient

# Establish a connection
client                                    =
MongoClient("mongodb://your_host:your_por
t")

# Access a specific database
db = client["your_database"]

# Access a collection within the database
collection = db["tasks"]

# Fetch documents
```

```
tasks = collection.find()
for task in tasks:
    print(task)


# Close the connection
client.close()
```

3. **Connecting to SQL Databases in C#**:

   o For **SQL Server** or **MySQL**, C# provides libraries like **ADO.NET** or **Entity Framework** to connect and interact with databases.

Example of connecting to **SQL Server** using **ADO.NET**:

```csharp
using System;
using System.Data.SqlClient;

class Program
{
    static void Main(string[] args)
    {
        string connectionString =
"Server=your_server;Database=your_databas
e;User
Id=your_user;Password=your_password;";
```

```
        using (SqlConnection conn = new
SqlConnection(connectionString))
        {
            conn.Open();

            // Execute a query
            SqlCommand    cmd    =    new
SqlCommand("SELECT * FROM tasks", conn);
            SqlDataReader    reader    =
cmd.ExecuteReader();

            // Read and display data
            while (reader.Read())
            {

Console.WriteLine(reader["task_name"]);
            }
            reader.Close();
        }
    }
}
```

4. **Connecting to NoSQL Databases in C#:**

   o For **MongoDB**, C# provides the **MongoDB.Driver** package.

   Example of connecting to **MongoDB** in C#:

   csharp

```csharp
using MongoDB.Driver;
using System;

class Program
{
    static void Main(string[] args)
    {
        // Establish a connection
        var client = new
MongoClient("mongodb://your_host:your_por
t");

        // Access a database
        var database =
client.GetDatabase("your_database");

        // Access a collection
        var collection =
database.GetCollection<BsonDocument>("tas
ks");

        // Fetch documents
        var tasks = collection.Find(new
BsonDocument()).ToList();
        foreach (var task in tasks)
        {

Console.WriteLine(task["task_name"]);
```

157

```
        }
    }
}
```

Real-World Example: Building a Cross-Platform App with a Cloud Database Backend

Let's walk through an example where we build a **cross-platform task management app** with a cloud database backend. We'll use **MongoDB Atlas** (a cloud-hosted version of MongoDB) as the backend database and connect it to both a **Python backend** and a **C# mobile app** using **Xamarin**.

1. **Setting Up MongoDB Atlas**:
   - First, sign up for **MongoDB Atlas** and create a new cluster. MongoDB Atlas offers a cloud-hosted, managed MongoDB service that is fully scalable and secure.
   - Create a database called `task_manager` and a collection called `tasks`.

2. **Python Backend (Flask)**:
   - Create a simple backend in **Python** using **Flask** to serve data to the mobile app.

```python
python

from flask import Flask, jsonify
```

```python
from pymongo import MongoClient

app = Flask(__name__)

# Establish connection to MongoDB Atlas
client                                 =
MongoClient("mongodb+srv://your_user:your
_password@your_cluster.mongodb.net/test")
db = client.task_manager
tasks_collection = db.tasks

@app.route('/tasks', methods=['GET'])
def get_tasks():
    tasks = tasks_collection.find()
    task_list       =       [{"task_name":
task["task_name"],        "description":
task["description"]} for task in tasks]
    return jsonify(task_list)

if __name__ == '__main__':
    app.run(debug=True)
```

3. **C# Frontend (Xamarin)**:

   o In the **Xamarin mobile app**, you will use
   HttpClient to make GET requests to the Flask
   backend and display the task data.

```
csharp
```

159

```
using System;
using System.Net.Http;
using System.Threading.Tasks;
using Xamarin.Forms;
using Newtonsoft.Json;

public class TaskPage : ContentPage
{
    private ListView taskListView;

    public TaskPage()
    {
        taskListView = new ListView();
        Content = new StackLayout
        {
            Children = { taskListView }
        };
    }

    protected    override    async    void
OnAppearing()
    {
        base.OnAppearing();
        var tasks = await GetTasksAsync();
        taskListView.ItemsSource = tasks;
    }

    private    async    Task<List<Task>>
GetTasksAsync()
```

```
        {
                var client = new HttpClient();
                var     response     =     await
        client.GetStringAsync("http://your-flask-
        server-url/tasks");
                var             tasks         =
        JsonConvert.DeserializeObject<List<Task>>
        (response);
                return tasks;
            }
        }


        public class Task
        {
            public string TaskName { get; set; }
            public string Description { get; set;
        }
        }
```

4. **Testing and Deployment**:

   o Run the Flask backend locally or deploy it to a cloud service like **Heroku** or **AWS**. Make sure the mobile app can connect to the backend and display the task data.

   o Test the mobile app on both **Android** and **iOS** to ensure cross-platform functionality, using the same MongoDB Atlas database to synchronize tasks across both platforms.

Conclusion

Choosing the right database for your cross-platform app depends on factors like data structure, scalability, and consistency requirements. **SQL databases** like MySQL or PostgreSQL are ideal for applications requiring structured data and complex queries, while **NoSQL databases** like MongoDB are better suited for applications with unstructured data, scalability needs, and rapid development cycles. In this chapter, we've seen how to connect to both **SQL** and **NoSQL** databases from Python and C#, and we've walked through an example of building a cross-platform app using a **MongoDB Atlas** backend. By leveraging the power of cloud databases, you can ensure that your cross-platform applications are scalable, secure, and highly available.

CHAPTER 16

CONTINUOUS INTEGRATION AND CONTINUOUS DEPLOYMENT (CI/CD) FOR CROSS-PLATFORM APPS

The Role of CI/CD in Agile Development

Continuous Integration (CI) and **Continuous Deployment (CD)** are essential practices in modern software development, particularly in **Agile development**. They help teams automate the processes of testing, building, and deploying applications, leading to faster and more reliable releases.

1. **Continuous Integration (CI)**:
    o **CI** is the practice of merging code changes from multiple contributors into a shared repository frequently (at least once a day). Each integration is automatically built and tested, allowing teams to identify integration problems early.
    o In **Agile development**, CI aligns with the Agile principles of delivering small, frequent updates.

Developers can check in their code regularly and ensure that the app is always in a working state, ready for the next sprint or feature.

2. **Continuous Deployment (CD)**:

    o **CD** takes CI a step further by automating the deployment process. After the code passes integration tests, it is automatically deployed to production or staging environments.

    o In Agile development, **CD** ensures that features can be released quickly after development. Every successful build is considered potentially ready for production, which helps teams deliver new features and bug fixes to end-users rapidly.

3. **Benefits in Agile Development**:

    o **Faster Feedback**: CI/CD pipelines provide immediate feedback on code quality, helping developers identify and fix issues earlier in the development process.

    o **Better Collaboration**: By automating the integration and deployment processes, CI/CD fosters collaboration among team members. Developers can focus on writing code, while CI/CD takes care of the build and deployment.

    o **Higher Quality**: Automated tests in CI/CD pipelines help ensure that the codebase remains stable and functional as changes are introduced.

This reduces the likelihood of bugs reaching production.

- o **Streamlined Releases**: CI/CD makes it easier to release software in small, manageable chunks. This allows teams to ship incremental updates quickly and frequently, which is crucial in Agile environments where the focus is on delivering working software early and often.

Setting Up CI/CD Pipelines for Python and C# Projects

Setting up CI/CD pipelines for your Python and C# projects helps automate the process of building, testing, and deploying your cross-platform applications. Here's how to set up pipelines for both Python and C# projects:

1. **Setting Up CI/CD for Python Projects**:
   - o Tools like **GitHub Actions**, **Travis CI**, or **CircleCI** can be used to set up CI/CD pipelines for Python applications.

   Example using **GitHub Actions** for a Python project:

   - o **Step 1**: Create a `.github/workflows/ci.yml` file in the root of your repository to define the CI/CD workflow.

```yaml
yaml

name: Python CI/CD Workflow

on:
  push:
    branches:
      - main
  pull_request:
    branches:
      - main

jobs:
  build:
    runs-on: ubuntu-latest

    steps:
      - name: Checkout code
        uses: actions/checkout@v2

      - name: Set up Python
        uses: actions/setup-python@v2
        with:
          python-version: '3.9'

      - name: Install dependencies
        run: |
          python -m pip install --upgrade pip
```

```
pip install -r requirements.txt

- name: Run tests
  run: |
    pytest   --maxfail=1   --disable-
warnings -q
```

- o **Step 2**: Define the stages in the YAML file:
  - **Checkout**: This step checks out the code from the repository.
  - **Set up Python**: This step sets up the Python environment.
  - **Install dependencies**: Install all the dependencies listed in `requirements.txt`.
  - **Run tests**: Runs the tests using `pytest` to ensure the code is functioning correctly.

2. **Setting Up CI/CD for C# Projects**:
   - o For C# projects, **GitHub Actions**, **Azure DevOps**, or **Jenkins** can be used to set up CI/CD pipelines.

Example using **GitHub Actions** for a C# project:

- o **Step 1**: Create a `.github/workflows/dotnet.yml` file in the root of your repository.

167

```yaml
yaml

name: .NET CI/CD Workflow

on:
  push:
    branches:
      - main
  pull_request:
    branches:
      - main

jobs:
  build:
    runs-on: ubuntu-latest

    steps:
      - name: Checkout code
        uses: actions/checkout@v2

      - name: Set up .NET
        uses: actions/setup-dotnet@v1
        with:
          dotnet-version: '5.0'

      - name: Restore dependencies
        run: dotnet restore

      - name: Build the project
```

```
        run: dotnet build --configuration
Release

    - name: Run tests
        run: dotnet test --configuration
Release

    - name: Publish
        run:    dotnet    publish    --
configuration Release --output ./publish

    - name: Deploy to Production
        run: |
        # Deploy your application here,
e.g., to server, use Azure CLI, etc.
        echo    "Deploying    app    to
production..."
```

   o **Step 2**: Define stages in the YAML file:

   ▪ **Checkout**: Checks out the code from the
      repository.

   ▪ **Set up .NET**: Sets up the .NET
      environment.

   ▪ **Restore dependencies**: Restores project
      dependencies.

   ▪ **Build the project**: Builds the project in
      the Release configuration.

- **Run tests**: Runs unit tests using `dotnet test`.
- **Publish**: Publishes the app to an output directory.
- **Deploy**: Deploys the app to the desired production environment (e.g., via Azure, AWS, or a custom server).

3. **Deploying Cross-Platform Apps**:

   o For **mobile apps** (using Xamarin), you may also want to include deployment steps for both **Android** and **iOS** in the CI/CD pipeline. This can be done by integrating mobile build tools such as **App Center** (for both iOS and Android) or **Fastlane** for automating builds and deployments.

   o For **backend** APIs, deployment to services like **AWS**, **Azure**, or **Heroku** can be included in the pipeline. Each platform typically provides CLI tools that can be used in the pipeline for deployment.

Real-World Example: Automating Deployments for Cross-Platform Mobile Apps

Let's walk through an example where we set up a CI/CD pipeline to automate deployments for a **cross-platform**

mobile app using **Xamarin** (C#) and deploy it to the **Google Play Store** and **Apple App Store** using **App Center**.

1. **Set Up App Center for Xamarin App**:
   - **Microsoft App Center** offers a complete CI/CD solution for mobile apps. It allows you to automatically build, test, distribute, and monitor apps.
   - Create an account on **App Center** and set up your project.
   - Connect your GitHub (or other Git repositories) to App Center.

2. **Configure CI/CD Pipeline in App Center**:
   - In App Center, create a new build pipeline for your Xamarin app.
   - Set up **build triggers** (e.g., when a commit is pushed to the `main` branch).
   - App Center will automatically build the app, run unit tests, and deploy to a **test group** or directly to the **Google Play Store** or **Apple App Store**.

3. **Configure Deployment to App Stores**:
   - To deploy to the **Google Play Store**:
     - Set up the **Google Play API** credentials in App Center.
     - In the App Center **distribution** settings, select the **Google Play** distribution group

and choose the specific release track (e.g., **Alpha, Beta**, or **Production**).

- o To deploy to the **Apple App Store**:
  - Set up the **App Store Connect API** credentials.
  - In App Center, choose **App Store Connect** for iOS and configure the pipeline for deployment.

4. **Example App Center CI/CD YAML File** (for **Xamarin.Android**):

```yaml

version: 1.0
apps:
  - name: MyXamarinApp
    platform: android
    steps:
      - name: Install dependencies
        run: |
            nuget restore MyXamarinApp.sln
      - name: Build the project
        run: |
            msbuild        MyXamarinApp.sln
/p:Configuration=Release
      - name: Test the project
        run: |
```

```
        # Run tests here, e.g., using
Xamarin.UITest
      - name: Deploy to Google Play Store
        run: |
          # Deploy APK to Google Play Store
using App Center
```

5. **Test and Monitor the Pipeline**:

   o Once set up, App Center will automatically trigger the build and deployment process whenever code is pushed to the repository. You can monitor the status of each step in the App Center dashboard and ensure that all builds, tests, and deployments run smoothly.

Conclusion

CI/CD plays a vital role in Agile development by enabling rapid, reliable, and automated builds, tests, and deployments. By setting up CI/CD pipelines for both **Python** and **C#** projects, you ensure that every change is tested and deployed efficiently across multiple platforms. In the real-world example of automating deployments for a **cross-platform mobile app**, tools like **App Center** can streamline the entire process, from building the app to testing and deploying to the **Google Play Store** and **Apple App Store**. With CI/CD, teams can focus on writing code and delivering features, while the pipeline ensures that everything else happens seamlessly and automatically.

CHAPTER 17

BUILDING SCALABLE CLOUD-BASED APPLICATIONS

Best Practices for Scaling Cloud Applications

Building scalable cloud-based applications is essential to ensuring that your application can handle increasing amounts of traffic, data, and users. Here are some best practices for scaling cloud applications:

1. **Leverage Cloud Auto-Scaling**:
   o   Cloud platforms like **AWS**, **Azure**, and **Google Cloud** offer **auto-scaling** features that automatically adjust resources (e.g., server instances) based on demand. This ensures that your application has enough resources to handle traffic spikes without over-provisioning.
   o   **Best Practice**: Set up auto-scaling based on metrics such as CPU usage, memory usage, or the number of incoming requests to ensure that resources scale up or down in real-time.

2. **Use Load Balancing**:

- o **Load balancers** distribute incoming traffic across multiple servers or instances, helping to avoid bottlenecks and ensuring high availability.
- o **Best Practice**: Use cloud-native load balancing services (e.g., **AWS Elastic Load Balancer**, **Azure Load Balancer**) to evenly distribute traffic and ensure optimal performance.

3. **Implement Caching**:

- o **Caching** is critical for performance and scalability. Caching reduces the number of repeated computations and database queries by storing frequently accessed data in memory.
- o **Best Practice**: Use a caching layer, such as **Redis** or **Memcached**, to store API responses, database query results, or session data, and reduce the load on your database.

4. **Database Sharding and Partitioning**:

- o As your data grows, a single database instance may become a bottleneck. **Database sharding** and **partitioning** involve splitting your data across multiple databases or tables to distribute the load.
- o **Best Practice**: Use **horizontal scaling** of databases by distributing data across multiple nodes. This approach helps handle large amounts of data and ensures high availability.

176

5. **Microservices Architecture**:
   o **Microservices** architecture involves breaking down a monolithic application into smaller, independent services, each responsible for a specific functionality (e.g., user management, payment processing, notifications). Each microservice can be scaled independently, providing greater flexibility and scalability.
   o **Best Practice**: Implement microservices with **containerization** tools like **Docker** and **Kubernetes** to ensure easy scaling, deployment, and management of your services.

6. **Use Content Delivery Networks (CDNs)**:
   o A **CDN** helps distribute static content (images, videos, stylesheets, etc.) across multiple geographically distributed servers, reducing latency and improving load times for users worldwide.
   o **Best Practice**: Use cloud-native CDN solutions like **AWS CloudFront** or **Azure CDN** to ensure your content is cached closer to the user, improving performance and reducing server load.

7. **Asynchronous Processing**:
   o Offload time-consuming tasks to **background workers** instead of performing them synchronously within the main application flow.

This ensures that your application remains responsive and scalable.

- o **Best Practice**: Use **message queues** (e.g., **Amazon SQS**, **RabbitMQ**) for asynchronous processing and decouple tasks such as email sending, image processing, or report generation from the main application.

8. **Monitor and Optimize Performance**:

- o **Monitoring** and **analytics** are essential for scaling cloud-based applications. Monitoring tools track system performance, server health, and resource utilization, while analytics help identify bottlenecks and areas for optimization.

- o **Best Practice**: Use cloud-native monitoring services like **AWS CloudWatch**, **Azure Monitor**, or **Google Cloud Monitoring** to track performance and proactively address potential scalability issues.

Using Microservices Architecture in Cross-Platform Projects

Microservices architecture allows you to break down a large application into smaller, independent services that communicate over APIs. This architecture is especially beneficial for cross-platform projects as it enables scaling individual services without impacting the entire application.

1. **Advantages of Microservices**:
   o **Independently Scalable**: Each microservice can be scaled independently based on its specific needs (e.g., if one microservice handles more traffic than others, it can be scaled up without affecting the other services).
   o **Technology Agnostic**: Each microservice can be developed using different technologies, making it easier to select the best tools for each service's specific requirements. For example, a user authentication service might be built with **Python** (Flask), while a payment processing service might be built with **C#** (ASP.NET Core).
   o **Resilience**: If one microservice fails, the others can continue to function. This makes the application more resilient and fault-tolerant.
   o **Faster Development and Deployment**: Microservices allow teams to work on different services simultaneously, speeding up development. Each service can be deployed independently, enabling continuous delivery and faster releases.

2. **Challenges with Microservices**:
   o **Increased Complexity**: Microservices introduce complexities in service communication, deployment, and management. Tools like **Docker**

and **Kubernetes** can help manage this complexity.

- o **Data Consistency**: With multiple microservices, ensuring **data consistency** across services can be challenging. You can use techniques like **event sourcing** or **saga pattern** to maintain consistency.
- o **Latency**: Communication between microservices can introduce network latency, so it's important to optimize communication patterns (e.g., synchronous vs. asynchronous) and ensure that services communicate efficiently.

Real-World Example: Building a Scalable Cross-Platform App in the Cloud

Let's walk through a real-world example of building a scalable **task management cross-platform app** using **microservices architecture** and **cloud infrastructure**.

Step 1: Architecture Overview

The app allows users to create, update, and delete tasks, and it has the following components:

1. **Frontend**: A cross-platform mobile app built with **Xamarin** for both iOS and Android.

180

2. **Backend**: A cloud-based backend using **microservices** hosted on **AWS** (Amazon Web Services).

3. **Microservices**:

   o **User Service**: Handles user authentication and profiles.

   o **Task Service**: Manages tasks, including CRUD operations.

   o **Notification Service**: Sends push notifications for task reminders.

4. **Cloud Infrastructure**: The app uses **AWS** services for hosting, scaling, and managing microservices.

Step 2: Setting Up Microservices

1. User Service (Authentication):

- The **User Service** is a microservice built with **Flask** (Python) that handles user authentication. It exposes APIs for registering, logging in, and managing user profiles.

- Use **JWT** (JSON Web Tokens) for stateless authentication, so that users don't need to log in repeatedly.

- This service is hosted on **AWS EC2** and can be scaled automatically based on incoming requests.

2. Task Service (Task Management):

- The **Task Service** is another microservice built with **ASP.NET Core** (C#) that manages task data. It provides APIs to create, update, retrieve, and delete tasks.
- The task data is stored in a **NoSQL** database like **MongoDB**, hosted on **AWS**.
- This service is also deployed to **AWS EC2**, and it is scaled independently from the User Service using **AWS Auto Scaling**.

3. Notification Service (Push Notifications):

- The **Notification Service** is built with **Node.js** and handles sending push notifications to users' devices when a task is due or when it's updated.
- It integrates with **Firebase Cloud Messaging** (FCM) for push notifications.
- This service is also deployed to **AWS EC2** and can scale independently.

Step 3: API Gateway and Load Balancer

To manage communication between microservices and to handle incoming requests, we use an **API Gateway** (e.g., **AWS API Gateway**) and **Load Balancer** (e.g., **AWS Elastic Load Balancer**):

- The **API Gateway** routes requests to the appropriate microservice (e.g., authentication requests go to the User Service, task-related requests go to the Task Service).
- The **Elastic Load Balancer** distributes incoming traffic evenly across the different instances of each microservice.

Step 4: Auto-Scaling and Caching

- **Auto-scaling** is set up for each microservice. For example, when the number of users increases, the **User Service** can automatically scale by adding more EC2 instances.
- **Redis** is used for caching frequently accessed data, such as user authentication tokens or the most recent tasks. This reduces load on the backend and speeds up response times.

Step 5: Continuous Integration and Continuous Deployment (CI/CD)

- **GitHub Actions** or **AWS CodePipeline** is used to automate the build, test, and deployment processes for each microservice.
- For example, when code is pushed to the GitHub repository, the CI pipeline runs tests, builds the microservice, and automatically deploys it to AWS EC2 using **Docker** containers.

Step 6: Monitoring and Logging

- **AWS CloudWatch** is used for monitoring the health of each microservice and auto-scaling events.
- **AWS X-Ray** provides distributed tracing to identify bottlenecks in communication between microservices.
- **Log aggregation** is set up using **AWS CloudWatch Logs** to collect logs from all microservices and provide insights into the system's behavior.

Step 7: Deploying the Cross-Platform Mobile App

The **Xamarin mobile app** interacts with the cloud-based microservices using REST APIs. The app is built and deployed using **Azure DevOps** or **App Center** and is distributed to both **Google Play** and the **Apple App Store**.

Conclusion:

By leveraging **microservices architecture**, cloud infrastructure (AWS), and best practices like **auto-scaling**, **CI/CD**, and **load balancing**, you can build a highly scalable, fault-tolerant, and performant **cross-platform app**. This architecture allows you to scale individual services independently, making the system more resilient and capable of handling growing traffic and user demands. This approach is ideal for applications with complex functionality and a need for continuous growth and flexibility.

CHAPTER 18

DEBUGGING AND TROUBLESHOOTING IN CROSS-PLATFORM DEVELOPMENT

Common Issues Faced in Cross-Platform Development

Cross-platform development allows you to write code once and deploy it across multiple platforms, but it also brings its own set of challenges. Here are some common issues that developers face in cross-platform development:

1. **Platform-Specific Bugs**:
   - Different platforms (iOS, Android, Windows, macOS) may behave differently due to variations in hardware, software, operating systems, and libraries. These discrepancies can result in bugs that only appear on certain platforms.
   - **Solution**: Use platform-specific code (e.g., conditional statements or platform-specific APIs) to handle differences. Be sure to test thoroughly on each platform.

2. **UI Inconsistencies**:

- o Ensuring a consistent user interface (UI) across different platforms can be difficult. While most frameworks (like **Xamarin**) allow you to design a single UI, differences in screen size, resolution, and platform guidelines can cause issues with layout and appearance.

- o **Solution**: Use responsive design principles, such as **flexible layouts** and **device-specific UI adjustments**, to ensure that your app looks and behaves consistently on different devices.

3. **Performance Variability**:

- o Performance can vary significantly across platforms. For example, an app might perform well on **iOS** but be slower on **Android** due to differences in how the operating systems manage resources.

- o **Solution**: Profile your app's performance on each platform and optimize resource usage (memory, CPU, etc.). Use platform-specific performance enhancements where needed.

4. **Third-Party Library Compatibility**:

- o Some libraries or APIs may only work on one platform or may require different implementations for each platform. This can result in inconsistencies or bugs when using shared libraries in cross-platform development.

- o **Solution**: Ensure the libraries you choose are cross-platform compatible, or use **dependency injection** to provide platform-specific implementations for different environments.

5. **Networking and API Issues**:
  - o Networking issues such as **latency**, **API inconsistencies**, and **data synchronization** can lead to problems, especially when the backend behaves differently depending on the platform.
  - o **Solution**: Test the network code thoroughly, use **asynchronous calls**, and ensure the backend APIs are designed for **platform-agnostic usage** (e.g., RESTful APIs).

Debugging Tools and Techniques for Python and C#

Both **Python** and **C#** provide powerful debugging tools and techniques for troubleshooting issues in cross-platform development. Here are some useful debugging tools and practices:

1. **Debugging in Python**:
  - o **Python Debugger (pdb)**: The built-in Python debugger, **pdb**, allows you to set breakpoints, step through code, and inspect

variables during runtime. You can use it as follows:

```
python
```

```
import pdb
pdb.set_trace()   # Set a breakpoint
```

Once the debugger hits the breakpoint, you can step through the code line by line, examine variables, and evaluate expressions.

o **IDE Debuggers**: Modern IDEs like **PyCharm**, **Visual Studio Code**, and **Eclipse** provide integrated debuggers for Python that offer graphical interfaces for stepping through code, inspecting variables, and viewing the call stack.

o **Logging**: Adding **logging** statements can help track the flow of your application and pinpoint where things go wrong. Use Python's built-in **logging** module:

```
python
```

```
import logging
```

```
logging.basicConfig(level=logging.D
EBUG)
logging.debug('This    is    a    debug
message')
```

o **Profiling Tools**: Use profiling tools like **cProfile** to analyze the performance of your Python code and identify bottlenecks.

```python
```

```
import cProfile
cProfile.run('your_function()')
```

2. **Debugging in C#**:

o **Visual Studio Debugger**: Visual Studio provides an excellent debugger for **C#** that allows you to set breakpoints, inspect variables, and step through code. It also supports **live debugging** for mobile applications built with **Xamarin**.

- You can set breakpoints directly in the code, and use the **Immediate Window** to evaluate expressions or change variable values during runtime.

o **Logging**: In C#, you can use the **NLog** or **Serilog** libraries to log messages at different levels (e.g., **Info**, **Debug**, **Error**). This helps in troubleshooting issues by providing insight into the application's behavior.

```csharp
using NLog;
var              logger              =
LogManager.GetCurrentClassLogger();
logger.Debug("This    is    a    debug
message");
```

o **Memory Profiling**: Tools like **dotMemory** or **Visual Studio Diagnostics Tools** can help identify memory leaks or inefficient memory usage in your C# applications.

o **Unit Testing and Mocking**: For isolating issues and ensuring that specific components of your app are working correctly, use **xUnit** or **NUnit** for unit testing. Additionally, **Moq** is a popular framework for mocking dependencies and testing interactions.

Real-World Example: Troubleshooting a Cross-Platform App with Performance Issues

Let's walk through a **real-world example** where we troubleshoot a **cross-platform task management app** that's experiencing performance issues. The app is built using **Xamarin (C#)** for the frontend and a **Python-based API** backend.

Step 1: Identify the Issue

Users report that the app is slow, especially when loading tasks from the backend or interacting with the UI. The performance issues are observed on both **Android** and **iOS**, but more pronounced on **Android**.

Step 2: Debugging the Backend (Python API)

We begin by debugging the **Python API**, as the frontend makes API calls to the backend to fetch task data.

1. **Use Profiling**:
   - Run **cProfile** on the task-fetching function to identify bottlenecks.

```
python
```

```
import cProfile
def fetch_tasks():
    # Code for fetching tasks from database
cProfile.run('fetch_tasks()')
```

- o The profiling results indicate that the **database query** is taking longer than expected.

2. **Optimize Database Queries**:
   - o We optimize the database query by adding **indexes** to frequently queried columns in the database (e.g., user_id and task_status).

3. **Add Caching**:
   - o We implement **Redis caching** for frequently accessed task data to reduce the load on the database and speed up response times.

```python
import redis
r = redis.StrictRedis(host='localhost', port=6379, db=0)
task_data = r.get('user_tasks')
if task_data is None:
    task_data = fetch_tasks_from_db()
    r.set('user_tasks', task_data, ex=300)
# Cache for 5 minutes
```

Step 3: Debugging the Frontend (Xamarin C# App)

After optimizing the backend, we focus on the **Xamarin mobile app** to troubleshoot any performance issues on the client-side.

1. **Use Xamarin Profiler**:
   - o We use the **Xamarin Profiler** to monitor memory usage and performance. The profiler helps identify areas where the app is consuming too much memory or processing power.
   - o The profiler shows that the **task list view** is being rendered inefficiently, leading to poor performance.
2. **Optimize UI Rendering**:
   - o We optimize the rendering of the task list by using **virtualization** for the list view, ensuring that only visible items are loaded and rendered, which reduces memory usage and improves performance.

```csharp
<ListView ItemsSource="{Binding TaskList}"
HasUnevenRows="True">
    <ListView.ItemTemplate>
```

```
<DataTemplate>
     <TextCell        Text="{Binding
TaskName}" />
     </DataTemplate>
   </ListView.ItemTemplate>
</ListView>
```

3. **Reduce API Calls**:
   - We optimize API calls by implementing **lazy loading** and **pagination** for task data. This reduces the amount of data requested from the server at once, improving both the network and UI performance.

4. **Use Asynchronous Calls**:
   - We ensure that all API calls are performed asynchronously, so the UI thread is not blocked while fetching tasks.

```csharp
var      tasks      =      await
apiClient.GetTasksAsync();
```

Step 4: Test and Monitor Performance

After implementing optimizations, we test the app on both **Android** and **iOS** to ensure that the performance issues have

195

been resolved. The app now loads tasks more quickly, and the UI remains responsive even with a large number of tasks.

We also continue monitoring the app in **production** using tools like **Firebase Analytics** and **Crashlytics** to track performance and detect any potential issues in real-time.

Conclusion

Debugging and troubleshooting in cross-platform development requires a systematic approach to identify performance issues and resolve them efficiently. In this example, we used a combination of **profiling, logging**, and **UI optimization techniques** to identify and fix performance issues in both the backend (Python API) and frontend (Xamarin app). Tools like **cProfile, Xamarin Profiler**, and **Redis caching** helped us optimize the app's performance, ensuring a smoother user experience across platforms. Debugging tools and practices like these are essential for delivering high-quality, performant cross-platform applications.

CHAPTER 19

DEPLOYING CROSS-PLATFORM APPLICATIONS TO MULTIPLE ENVIRONMENTS

Packaging Apps for Different Platforms (Windows, macOS, Linux, Android, iOS)

When developing cross-platform applications, packaging your app for different environments is crucial to ensure that the app runs smoothly on various operating systems and devices. Each platform has its own packaging requirements and tools, so you need to ensure that the app is prepared according to the guidelines for each environment.

1. **Packaging for Windows**:
   o For Windows applications, you may want to create a **.exe** installer or package your app as a **MSI** file for easy installation.
   o **For .NET Core (C#)** apps, you can use **Visual Studio** or **dotnet CLI** to publish your application:

   ```
   bash
   ```

```
dotnet publish -c Release -r win-x64
--self-contained
```

- o This will create a folder with all the necessary files, including the executable, that can be bundled into an installer.

2. **Packaging for macOS**:
   - o For macOS applications, you'll need to create a **.dmg** (Disk Image) or **.pkg** installer for distribution.
   - o For **Xamarin** apps or **.NET Core** applications, use **Visual Studio for Mac** to create a macOS package. You can also use **Electron** for creating cross-platform desktop apps that work on macOS.
   - o **Example**: Using **Electron** with **Node.js**, you can package and create installers for macOS.

   ```bash
   bash
   ```

   ```
   electron-packager  .  MyApp  --
   platform=darwin --arch=x64
   ```

3. **Packaging for Linux**:
   - o For Linux, you can package your application into **DEB** (Debian) or **RPM** (RedHat) packages or use

AppImage for distribution across different Linux distributions.

- o   For **C#** apps running on Linux, you can use the **dotnet CLI** to publish and package:

bash

```
dotnet publish -c Release -r linux-
x64 --self-contained
```

- o   For **Python apps**, create a **.tar.gz** or use **PyInstaller** to bundle your app with all its dependencies.

bash

```
pyinstaller --onefile myapp.py
```

4. **Packaging for Android**:

- o   Android apps built with **Xamarin** or **Java/Kotlin** require packaging into an **APK** (Android Package) file. You can use **Android Studio** or **Xamarin** to create the APK.
- o   **For Xamarin**:

bash

```
msbuild MyXamarinApp.csproj /t:Build
/p:Configuration=Release
/p:Platform=Android
```

- o You can also use **App Center** to automate the build and distribution process for **Android**.

5. **Packaging for iOS**:
    - o iOS apps need to be packaged as **IPA** (iOS App) files. This process requires a **Mac** environment with **Xcode**.
    - o **For Xamarin or .NET Core apps**, you can use **Xamarin Studio** or **Visual Studio for Mac** to package the iOS app into an IPA file. The app can then be distributed via the **App Store** or **TestFlight**.
    - o Use the following command to create an iOS app:

```
bash
```

```
msbuild MyXamarinApp.csproj /t:Build
/p:Configuration=Release
/p:Platform=iPhone
```

Deployment Strategies for Cloud and On-Premises Solutions

1. **Cloud Deployment**:
    - o **Cloud deployment** is ideal for apps that require scalability, reliability, and global

accessibility. Cloud providers like **AWS**, **Azure**, and **Google Cloud** offer various tools and services to deploy and manage applications.

- o **For Python Apps**:

  - **AWS Elastic Beanstalk** or **Google App Engine** are great for deploying Python web applications. You can package your Python app, upload it to the cloud platform, and let the service handle scaling and deployment.

  - Example using **AWS Elastic Beanstalk** for Python:

    ```bash
    eb init -p python-3.7 my-app
    eb create my-app-env
    eb deploy
    ```

  - This will deploy the Python app to AWS and handle scaling and load balancing automatically.

- o **For C# Apps**:

  - **Azure App Services** is a powerful service for deploying **ASP.NET Core** applications. You can deploy directly from **Visual Studio** or through **Azure CLI**.

- Example using **Azure CLI** for C#:

```bash

az webapp up --name my-app --resource-group my-resource-group --plan my-app-service-plan
```

- This will deploy your C# app to an Azure web app service, which automatically scales based on usage.

2. **On-Premises Deployment**:

   o For **on-premises deployment**, you will need to manage the infrastructure and ensure the app is hosted on your own servers or data centers. This is ideal for applications with strict regulatory or security requirements, such as in industries like finance or healthcare.

   o **For Python Apps**:

      - Use **Docker** containers to package your Python application, making it portable and easier to deploy across various environments. Deploy the Docker container to a **Docker Host** or **Kubernetes** cluster.

- Example using Docker:

```bash
docker build -t my-python-app
.
docker run -p 5000:5000 my-python-app
```

o **For C# Apps**:

- **Windows Server** or **Linux Server** can be used to host your **ASP.NET Core** applications. You can use **IIS** or **NGINX** as a reverse proxy for C# applications running in production environments.

- Example using **IIS**:

    - Publish the app using **Visual Studio** and then deploy the published files to the IIS server. Configure the IIS server to forward requests to the C# application.

*Real-World Example: Deploying a Python App to Cloud Services
and a C# App to Mobile*

Let's go through an example where we deploy a **Python app**
to the **cloud** and a **C# mobile app** to **Google Play** and **Apple
App Store**.

Step 1: Deploying the Python App to AWS

1. **Set Up AWS Elastic Beanstalk**:
   - First, ensure you have an **AWS account** and the
     AWS CLI installed.
   - Install **Elastic Beanstalk CLI** using:

   bash

   ```
   pip install awsebcli
   ```

2. **Prepare the Python App**:
   - Ensure that your Python app has a
     requirements.txt file for dependencies.

   bash

   ```
   Flask==2.0.1
   boto3==1.18.0
   ```

3. **Initialize Elastic Beanstalk**:

204

The Universal Developer's Guide

o   Navigate to your Python app directory and
    initialize Elastic Beanstalk:

```bash

eb init -p python-3.8 my-python-app
```

4. **Create and Deploy the Environment**:

    o   Create an environment and deploy your app:

```bash

eb create my-python-env
eb deploy
```

5. **Verify the Deployment**:

    o   After deployment, you can check the URL
        provided by AWS to ensure your Python app is
        live.

Step 2: Deploying the C# Mobile App to Google Play and Apple App Store

1. **Set Up App Center**:

    o   Create an **App Center** account and link your
        GitHub repository to App Center.

    o   Configure **build** settings for both **iOS** and
        Android.

2. **Build the Xamarin App**:

   o Use **Visual Studio** or **App Center** to build the app for **Android** and **iOS**.

   o Ensure that **App Center** is set up to automatically build the app whenever there is a new commit to the repository.

3. **Deploy the App to Google Play Store**:

   o Set up **Google Play Developer Console** and configure your app's distribution settings in **App Center**.

   o App Center will automatically deploy the app to the **Google Play Store** once the build is completed.

4. **Deploy the App to Apple App Store**:

   o Set up **App Store Connect** and configure your app's distribution settings for **TestFlight** or the **App Store** in **App Center**.

   o App Center will automatically upload the app to **TestFlight** or **App Store** once the build is completed.

5. **Test the App**:

   o Test the Android app on **Google Play** and the iOS app via **TestFlight** or directly through the **App Store** to ensure everything works as expected.

Conclusion

Deploying cross-platform applications to multiple environments involves ensuring that each platform and cloud service is properly configured for the specific application needs. Packaging apps for different platforms, using cloud or on-premises deployment strategies, and automating deployments through tools like **AWS Elastic Beanstalk** for Python apps and **App Center** for C# mobile apps help streamline the process. This approach ensures that your applications are scalable, reliable, and ready for production on any platform. By following the steps outlined in the real-world example, you can deploy a **Python app to cloud services** and a **C# app to mobile platforms**, making your applications available to users across different environments.

CHAPTER 20

LOOKING AHEAD: THE FUTURE OF CROSS-PLATFORM DEVELOPMENT, AGILE, AND CLOUD INTEGRATION

Emerging Trends in Cross-Platform Development

Cross-platform development has evolved significantly over the past few years, and the future holds even more exciting possibilities. As technology continues to advance, developers are embracing new tools, platforms, and methodologies that make building scalable, efficient, and feature-rich applications across multiple platforms easier and faster. Here are some key **emerging trends** in cross-platform development:

1. **Unified Development Environments**:
   - Tools and frameworks like **Flutter**, **React Native**, and **Xamarin** have revolutionized the ability to build cross-platform applications by providing a unified development environment for both iOS and Android.

- o The trend toward **single-codebase frameworks** is accelerating, reducing development time, complexity, and maintenance costs.
- o In the future, we can expect even more powerful and seamless frameworks that support not only mobile platforms but also **desktop** and **web applications** from the same codebase.

2. **WebAssembly (Wasm)**:

- o **WebAssembly (Wasm)** is gaining traction as a cross-platform solution for building performance-optimized web apps that run natively on the browser. It allows developers to compile code written in languages like **C**, **C++**, and **Rust** to run in the browser with near-native performance.
- o In the future, **Wasm** may be used to enable cross-platform capabilities beyond traditional web apps, allowing applications to be developed once and run on almost any device with a browser.

3. **Progressive Web Apps (PWAs)**:

- o **PWAs** are a blend of web and mobile apps, providing users with a native-like experience on their devices while being developed and deployed through web technologies like **HTML**, **CSS**, and **JavaScript**.

- With the rise of mobile-first development and **web standards** improving, PWAs are becoming increasingly powerful, making them a compelling solution for cross-platform development that minimizes the need for separate native apps.

4. **Low-Code and No-Code Platforms**:
   - Low-code and no-code platforms are making it easier for non-developers and citizen developers to create cross-platform applications. Tools like **OutSystems**, **Mendix**, and **Appgyver** allow rapid application development (RAD) without the need to write extensive code.
   - In the future, we can expect more sophisticated tools to bridge the gap between developers and non-developers, allowing everyone to contribute to the development of cross-platform applications.

5. **Enhanced Integration with Cloud and Microservices**:
   - The future of cross-platform development will be more tightly integrated with cloud-based infrastructure and **microservices architecture**. With **serverless computing**, **API-first design**, and **edge computing**, developers will be able to build scalable and performant applications that are deeply integrated with the cloud.

- o Cloud providers like **AWS**, **Azure**, and **Google Cloud** are expanding their cross-platform capabilities, offering increasingly robust services for building cloud-native apps that work seamlessly across multiple platforms.

The Growing Role of AI and Machine Learning in Development

The integration of **artificial intelligence (AI)** and **machine learning (ML)** in development is a rapidly growing trend that will shape the future of cross-platform applications. AI and ML are transforming how applications are built, deployed, and interacted with, and this transformation is only going to accelerate in the coming years. Here's how AI and ML are influencing the future of cross-platform development:

1. **AI-Powered Development Tools**:
   - o AI is playing an increasingly important role in the development lifecycle itself. Tools like **GitHub Copilot** are leveraging AI to provide real-time code suggestions and automating parts of the coding process, improving productivity and reducing the time developers spend on routine tasks.

o **AI-based testing tools** are also gaining popularity, where ML algorithms automatically detect bugs, security vulnerabilities, and performance bottlenecks in code.

2. **Intelligent User Interfaces**:

o AI is powering **intelligent UIs**, enabling voice commands, gesture recognition, natural language processing (NLP), and more. AI-driven personalization and recommendation engines are being embedded into apps to create dynamic user experiences that adapt based on user preferences.

o In cross-platform development, AI will help build more responsive and personalized user interfaces that can adapt across devices, making the experience feel more cohesive.

3. **Automating Deployment and Scaling with AI**:

o AI is already starting to influence **cloud deployments**. In the future, AI could play a larger role in automatically scaling applications, detecting performance issues, and providing automated performance optimization across cloud-based environments. This will be particularly valuable for cross-platform apps that need to run on different devices and networks.

4. **AI for Data Analytics and Insights**:

212

- o Many cross-platform applications are integrating AI to process vast amounts of data. For example, apps using AI-powered **analytics** can provide deep insights into user behavior, helping businesses make more informed decisions.
- o **Predictive analytics** and **recommendation systems** are becoming more common in apps that rely on big data and machine learning models to provide personalized content or predictions.

5. **AI-Driven APIs and Services**:

- o Cloud providers are offering AI and ML services through **APIs**, which makes it easier for developers to integrate AI capabilities into cross-platform apps. These include services for **image recognition**, **speech-to-text**, **sentiment analysis**, and more.
- o These AI-powered APIs allow developers to add advanced features without needing to build complex models from scratch.

Real-World Example: Preparing a Cross-Platform App for AI Integration

Let's walk through an example of preparing a **cross-platform task management app** for **AI integration**. The app is built with **Xamarin** (C#) for mobile platforms (iOS and Android) and a **Python backend** with AI-powered features.

Step 1: Identify the AI Features to Integrate

We decide to integrate the following AI-powered features into the app:

- **AI-powered Task Prioritization**: Using a machine learning model to suggest the priority of tasks based on user behavior, due dates, and task history.
- **Speech-to-Text**: Allow users to add tasks by speaking, using **speech recognition**.
- **Personalized Recommendations**: Suggest tasks or content based on the user's activity and preferences using **machine learning**.

Step 2: Integrating AI into the Python Backend

1. **AI-Powered Task Prioritization**:
   - We train a **machine learning model** (using **scikit-learn** or **TensorFlow**) to predict the priority of tasks based on features like task due date, time of day, and task history.
   - Once the model is trained, we expose an API endpoint using **Flask** to send task data and receive prioritization suggestions.

Example of an AI API endpoint in Python (Flask):

```python
python

from flask import Flask, request, jsonify
from sklearn.externals import joblib

app = Flask(__name__)

# Load the pre-trained ML model
model                                  =
joblib.load('task_priority_model.pkl')

@app.route('/predict', methods=['POST'])
def predict():
    task_data = request.json
    # Process the task data and predict
priority
    priority                           =
model.predict([task_data['features']])
    return              jsonify({"priority":
priority[0]})

if __name__ == '__main__':
    app.run(debug=True)
```

2. **Integrating Speech-to-Text**:
   o We use **Google Cloud Speech-to-Text API** to convert voice input into text.

215

- In the **Xamarin** mobile app, we integrate the Google Speech SDK and send the recorded audio to the Python backend for processing.

Example (C# Xamarin Speech-to-Text):

```csharp
var      speechRecognizer      =      new
SpeechRecognizer();
var      result      =      await
speechRecognizer.RecognizeAsync();
string taskDescription = result.Text;
```

Step 3: Integrating AI into the Xamarin Mobile App

1. **Request AI Predictions**:
   - From the mobile app, we call the Python backend's API endpoint to get task prioritization suggestions:

```csharp
HttpClient client = new HttpClient();
var      response      =      await
client.PostAsJsonAsync("https://yourbacke
nd.com/predict", taskData);
```

```
var          priority          =          await
response.Content.ReadAsAsync<PriorityResp
onse>();
```

2. **Display Prioritized Tasks**:
   - o Once the mobile app receives the priority from the AI model, it updates the task list to show the tasks in priority order.

3. **Voice Input for Adding Tasks**:
   - o Users can add tasks by speaking. The app uses **Google's Speech-to-Text API** to convert voice into text, which is then saved as a new task in the backend.

   Example of task creation with voice:

   csharp

```
var task = new Task { Description =
taskDescription, Priority = priority };
await apiClient.CreateTaskAsync(task);
```

Step 4: Continuous Improvement with Machine Learning

- As users interact with the app, we collect data on their task priorities and behaviors. This data can be used to **retrain** the machine learning model periodically to improve accuracy and provide better suggestions over time.

- We can use **cloud services** like **AWS Sagemaker**, **Google AI**, or **Azure Machine Learning** to automate the retraining process.

Conclusion

The future of cross-platform development is incredibly exciting, with the integration of **AI** and **machine learning** opening up new possibilities for creating smarter, more personalized applications. In this chapter, we've explored how to integrate AI-powered features such as **task prioritization**, **speech-to-text**, and **personalized recommendations** into a **cross-platform mobile app**. By combining **cloud-based AI services**, **machine learning models**, and **cross-platform frameworks** like **Xamarin** and **Python**, we can create powerful applications that adapt to user needs and continuously improve over time. The ability to seamlessly integrate AI into cross-platform apps will undoubtedly become a key driver of innovation in the development landscape.

www.ingramcontent.com/pod-product-compliance
Lightning Source LLC
LaVergne TN
LVHW051325050326
832903LV00031B/3378